FIXING ILLINOIS

FIXING ILLINOIS

Politics and Policy in the Prairie State

JAMES D. NOWLAN AND J. THOMAS JOHNSON

UNIVERSITY OF ILLINOIS PRESS

Urbana, Chicago, and Springfield

Library of Congress Control Number: 2014934783
ISBN 978-0-252-07996-2 (paperback)
ISBN 978-0-252-09635-8 (e-book)

Contents

Illustrations

-

TABLES

FIGURES

Acknowledgments

We begin by acknowledging major financial support from the Illinois Fiscal Policy Council, the 501(c)(3) education and research affiliate of the Taxpayers' Federation of Illinois, without which this project would not have been possible.

David Yepsen, director of the Paul Simon Public Policy Institute at Southern Illinois University, and Ronald Michaelson, visiting professor of political science at the University of Illinois, Springfield, read an early draft of the manuscript and made numerous important criticisms and suggestions that have improved the final product significantly. Zachary Stamp and Gary Koch, both longtime observers of Illinois government and politics, also read the complete manuscript in draft form and contributed materially to the final product.

We could not have written the chapter on infrastructure without the knowledge and guidance of Linda Wheeler, retired director of policy and planning at the Illinois Department of Transportation, although the recommendations in the chapter, as throughout the book, are the authors' alone.

Jim Nowlan thanks Len (Rob) Small, president of the Small Newspaper Group, for permission to draw excerpts from Nowlan's weekly columns in that chain of newspapers for inclusion in the book. In addition, Janet Kamerer and the staff at the Toulon Public Library did a terrific job of procuring books through interlibrary loan for Jim Nowlan's use.

Others with whom we have talked and from whom we learned include, in alphabetical order, Frank Beal, Less Boucher, Bob Brock, Kirsten Carroll, Lori Clark, Michael Clark, Linda Daley, Natalie Davila, Kurt DeWeese, Theresa Eagleson, Sue Ebetsch, Josh Evans, Julie Farmer, Randy Fritz, Raul Garza, Julie Hamos, Daniel Hankiewicz, John Hartnett, Adam Horst, George Hovanec, Loren Iglarsh, Jonathan Ingram, Jeff Johnson, Cristopher Johnston, Robert Kaestner, Lynnae Kapp, Gene Keefe, Richard King, Robert Kjellander, Mike Klemens, Clayton Klenke, Representative David Leitch, Ann Louisin, Debra Matlock, Jeff Mays, Steve McClure, Jess McDonald, Dea Meyer, Ron Michaelson, Rich Miller, Fred Montgomery, Don Moss, Patrick Mullen, Nancy Nelson, Stephen Newell, Nick Palazzolo, Howard Peters, Jon Pickering, Lance Pressl, Robert Powers, Kristina Rasmussen, Mary Barber Reynolds, Robert Rich, Gail Ripka, Jan Sams, Steve Sams, Marvin Schaar, Gregg Scott, Jay Dee Shattuck, Eric Shields, Charles Snyder, Jeff Stauter, Senator Heather Steans, Janelle Steffen, Carl Stover, Janet Stover, Kara Teeple, David Tretter, Don Udstuen, and Dick Westfall. The authors apologize to any contributors whose names have been inadvertently left off this list.

Kellie Cookson and Courtney Flanders at the Illinois Fiscal Policy Council in Springfield provided invaluable support in the preparation of the manuscript. We also thank Willis Regier, director of the University of Illinois Press, for his support and guidance throughout the project. In addition, Jane Zanichkowsky did a superb job of editing the final manuscript that has improved the clarity and readability of the book markedly.

The many suggestions made in the following chapters, as well as errors of fact and interpretation, are those of the authors alone.

Preface

The purpose of this small book is to contribute to a rebuilding of public confidence and trust in Illinois governments, in particular, its state government. The book is an overview of Illinois and its government by two fellows who have each participated in and observed Illinois policymaking for more than four decades. Our book takes a look back, discusses the present state of affairs, and offers policy suggestions and recommendations that we believe could lead overall to a more positive future for our state, for which we have deep affection.

Illinois has been going through a rough patch. In recent years successive governors have been convicted of political crimes. For a while, the state was the butt of jokes on late night television shows about one of these, the eccentric Rod Blagojevich, and the perceived corrupt nature of the state generally.

Further, the state has been struggling under a mountain of debt and unfunded pension and healthcare obligations. In 2011 the state individual income tax was increased by two-thirds, to a rate of 5 percent, in order to address an unbalanced budget and up to $8 billion in unpaid bills. Finally, on this short list of problems bedeviling the state, is the fact that Illinois residents continue to leave the state in greater numbers than people coming in. This net outmigration has plagued the state since at least 1965 and is a cause of its slow population growth in recent decades.

Yet, as the reader will see, the state has great strengths—infrastructure, location, an educated workforce, Chicago, and copious amounts of water.

This book is not meant to be comprehensive, definitive, or conclusive. Instead, we see it as a starting point in a substantive discussion during an important election year, a discussion of the sort that is too often lacking in election years. We do believe that the many suggestions and recommendations we lay out in boldface in the ensuing chapters merit consideration and are worthy of broad discussion. If some, or many, of them are ultimately found wanting, then the discussion they generated still might lead to more effective options.

Some of our recommendations would be difficult to enact and implement, especially in the political sphere, because of inertia and because some options might create winners but also losers.

The authors are philosophically moderate. Some of our options might be cheered by conservatives, others by liberals. Our overall tendencies are pragmatic, we think.

In addition to chapters about the major policy areas of taxing and spending, education, health care and human services, infrastructure, economic development, and reengineering of state government, we also discuss corruption, a topic that we believe is important to Illinois's future but one in which state government's role is less direct and more limited.

Please join us in a substantive discussion of steps that can be taken to fulfill the promise of Illinois. Readers with questions or suggestions may contact us at jnowlan3@gmail.com and tom@iltaxwatch.org.

FIXING ILLINOIS

The Future of Illinois

When we were boys growing up in small-town Illinois in the 1950s, life was good, and getting better. Crops on the farms around us were growing in size each year, and we saw trucks go through town loaded with hogs or cattle, headed for the sprawling Chicago Stock Yards, then to be cut into bacon and steaks at the great meat packers in the city.

Chicago was far distant for us boys, yet we knew the city was big enough to host our favorite baseball and football teams. And we had seen pictures of the city's factories, belching smoke and producing steel and appliances that our parents were becoming prosperous enough to buy.

We were proud to be from Illinois.

Today, many if not most of us are in a funk about our state. For a while, as the political career of former governor Rod Blagojevich unraveled, Illinois was the butt of jokes, which only accentuated our state's reputation for corruption. About the same time, Illinois was becoming a focus of attention for being a deadbeat state, unable to pay its bills on time. We raised taxes and still could not restore stability to our state budget. Our credit rating is the lowest in the country and our business climate is abysmal. An exodus of people from Illinois that began decades ago continues.

We wince when traveling out of state to hear people making light jokes about our state or asking pointed questions about what is going on in Illinois. According to one national public opinion survey, Illinois is the second most disliked state in the nation, after California. That is, significantly more people have negative thoughts about Illinois than favorable ones.[1] Things are not good in Illinois, and they don't appear to be getting better.

Yet Illinois still has the strengths that made it great. Most states would be envious of what Illinois has. We have a prime location in the center of the country, and most markets are but a day away on our unparalleled infrastructure of interstates, rail, air, and water. Most parts of Illinois have plenty of underground or surface water. In Chicago we have a leading metropolitan region with global reach. Our system of higher education has been strong, and the state is above average in per capita wealth.

But we lack a plan for lifting our state out of its problems. Instead, we lurch ahead from year to year, unsure of where to go, struggling to get our heads above water.

We need a multi-year plan for restoring stability to our finances, without driving more people from our state, and then a plan for investment in infrastructure, our crown jewel, and in our schools, which include a mix of the very good, the mediocre, and the very bad.

We can, however, pull out of our funk and use our strengths to become a state in which, once again, we can be proud. In this book we have identified suggestions for change that could put us back on a path to stability and prosperity.

First, we must put our fiscal house in order. Doing so will require action to reduce our long-term pension obligations and hold growth in Medicaid expenditures to no more than the rate of inflation. Our pension obligations have grown to unsustainable levels as a result of habitual underfunding combined with increases in benefits over the years. In order to save the pension systems, painful concessions will be needed from current employees and retirees. We must also shift responsibilities for pensions from the state to the governments that incur them—that is, our school districts and public universities. In December 2013, the Illinois General Assembly and governor enacted significant changes in the Illinois pension programs. As of press time, the Illinois Supreme Court had not ruled on the constitutionality of the new law.

As for Medicaid, no one appears to have found a way to level off costs of health care. We propose that participants become more responsible for their own health care, through wellness programs and efforts at cessation of unhealthful conditions such as obesity and practices such as smoking. Those who fail to try to adopt healthful ways will have to be sanctioned with increased co-payments. We also think serious consideration should be given to an insurance voucher program for Medicaid recipients, a proposition that, proponents believe, can cut costs significantly. The healthcare delivery system also has to be reformed, so that there is less use of the expensive emergency room and so that there are more resources for care at home, rather than in a nursing home.

Without strong actions with regard to pensions and Medicaid, there is little hope of restoring stability to our state budget.

On the revenue side of the budget coin, we should reduce our corporate income tax rate, which is one of the highest in the country. If it is deemed necessary to find additional revenue to offset this reduction, we should definitely not raise other rates but instead broaden the base of existing taxes. For example, our sales tax base is very narrow and focused on goods, where growth in sales is slow, and not on services, where growth is faster. Our state income tax also has a somewhat narrow base, with retirement income completely exempted and a 5 percent credit on property taxes paid, which few link in their minds to property tax relief. By broadening the bases of our major taxes, we could even lower the overall tax rates.

After Medicaid, education is the largest expenditure in the budget (it was always the biggest expenditure until Medicaid costs surpassed those of education many years ago). Here we are mired in the middle in terms of standard test achievement scores. Yet these averages often hide more than they reveal. Many suburban schools in prosperous communities are quite good. Because the funding system is based on property wealth, these schools spend more per pupil than do other schools but in addition, the families in prosperous suburbs have higher educational expectations for their children, which is more important, we believe, than the money.

Still, there are many rural and urban districts where per pupil spending is less robust and where parental and community expectations are far too modest. Schools must play a part in building expectations for success. In the meantime, we should increase the length of the school day and school year, to be more in line with other developed and rapidly developing nations. Further, we should create a new year-round school calendar, with breaks shorter than the traditional summer-long break, when so much learning is lost.

Higher education in Illinois, and elsewhere, must reinvent itself. Rapidly increasing tuition and room and board costs have been putting traditional four-year college out of reach of many parents, and no longer can students work their way through college. Students in increasing numbers are turning to community colleges as the springboard to their higher education. And more four-year colleges are offering their third year on community college campuses, which also helps with costs.

Online higher education is also in vogue, and students are becoming comfortable learning in that way. Massive open online courses (MOOCs) are all the rage at present. Faculty from top universities offer online instruction that is, at present, free, but will someday have to cost something, though probably much less than at traditional brick-and-mortar colleges.

With different delivery systems for higher education developing, the state should rethink how it funds higher education. At present, public universities are funded through a formula based on enrollment, on the premise this can keep tuition somewhat lower than otherwise. We think that a partly market-driven funding approach should be taken. Instead of funding universities, we propose funding the student, who could in turn take his or her funding to whatever delivery system offered the most value for the dollar. This should force public and private colleges to be as efficient and worthy as possible, in order to attract the students' dollars.

Funding for human services represents the next largest slice of the state budget. It is aimed, for example, at people with mental, physical, and developmental problems, children who are troubled or who have lost their parents to dysfunction, and the elderly. We don't do as good a job for them as we could, and much of the problem lies with antiquated information technology. Unfortunately, our many social service units operate within "silos"; that is, they cannot communicate digitally with one another. This creates problems for families that have members with more than one service need, who often do not know where to turn and who are often bounced from agency to agency.

Throughout state government, but especially in the human services, we must quickly replace multiple information technology (IT) platforms with integrated systems that can all follow the same patient. Part of the problem has been that individual agencies have funded their own IT systems from their respective operating budgets. With budgeting very tight in recent years, spending in this area has regularly been cut or eliminated. Since IT represents a long-term investment, the state should use capital construction bonds to provide the funding for the investments. The Quinn administration floated one bond issue of $25 million in 2012 for such purposes, and much more will need to be done to accomplish the major objectives set out here.

The business climate of the state is abysmal. National rankings of the state in this regard generally put the state in the bottom ten. The rankings measure different dimensions of our situation and may not be valid, yet they create the perception across the country that Illinois is not a place to start or expand a business. Several steps can be taken to change our image. We ought, first, to reduce the corporate income tax from 9.5 percent to no more than 7.3 percent, where it was until the 2011 tax increases, and second, develop a credible plan to get our fiscal house in order. Businesses are wary that they might be saddled, via future tax increases, with the responsibility for our unfunded pension liabilities and for erasing our unpaid bills of about $8 billion.

Third, we need to truly reform workers' compensation laws. The 2011 changes in these laws did not change the "causation standard," according to which the employer is responsible for the entire medical and disability costs of an injury, even if the workplace contributed nothing to the cause of an injury. All that lawyers for the injured have to do is persuade the arbitrators that the workplace "might have" or "could have been a contributor" to the injury, even if the injury occurred outside the workplace. This has led to gross abuse of the system and needs to be changed.

We have hundreds of economic development agencies across the state. Too often they compete against one another in a zero-sum game of simply moving companies and businesses around in the same state. Metropolitan Chicago should develop an overarching economic development unit, and Illinois should take the lead in creating a Global Midwest Forum, first proposed by Richard Longworth in his book, *Caught in the Middle*.[2] This forum could well be patterned after the Southern Regional Growth Board, which is based in the research triangle in North Carolina and in which the states' governors each chair a committee of the group.

The great mix of infrastructure is the crown jewel among our resources. Our rail and interstate highway systems are unmatched in the country; we have substantial airport and water transport resources. Yet we have no plan for maintaining and building on these advantages. Instead, we go from short-term plan to no plan for several years and then back to another short-term plan. We will need new funding sources based on such approaches as vehicle miles traveled and congestion pricing, these to supplement traditional revenues from motor fuel taxes, which are declining because of improved fuel efficiency.

The state can also manage itself more effectively. We should, for example, move from a paper-based cash accounting system to a digitally automated system. It is estimated this could generate about $200 million in one-time increased cash flow, according to a leading accountant in Illinois who has intimate knowledge of state finance. The state should also outsource management of its sprawling real estate assets and facilities maintenance. Further, we should reduce the numbers of nonviolent prisoners in our corrections system, where overall numbers have ballooned from 8,000 in 1970 to 49,000 in 2013. Many adults and juvenile inmates could be served better and less expensively in community-based mental health and substance abuse programs.

Corruption has been an enduring habit in Illinois. In a 2012 national opinion survey, Illinois was perceived to be the third most corrupt state in the nation.[3] The survey showed that our neighboring states were rarely noted for being corrupt, which means that we stand out like a sore thumb in the Midwest. The recent incarceration of two governors embarrassed Illinois residents. Fortunately, three in four Illinois residents, in yet another poll, disagreed with the statement "Nothing can be done about the corruption."[4]

This suggests that the public is ready for action. But of what kind? The next governor should create a permanent task force on changing the culture of corruption that, we think, has permeated the state over the decades. This should be a high-profile group that engages the public in an ongoing dialogue about the insidious corrosion that corruption works in a political system and of the role of an active citizenry in rejecting corruption. We have seen American culture change with regard to topics such as smoking and drinking and driving, so it can be done.

Further, we think that public financing of election campaigns should be enacted to provide pathways to election for candidates who are free from big campaign contributions. Finally, we believe that the drawing of state legislative districts should be done by a bipartisan commission, independent of the legislature. A petition drive is under way to put such a proposal on the ballot in November 2014.

The state is in a funk. The 2012 Illinois Policy Survey by Northern Illinois University found that seven in ten residents feel the state is headed in the wrong direction.[5] It does not have to be this way. In this book we suggest policies, processes, and management techniques, most borrowed from others plus a few of our own, that might help turn the state around over time. Some of our suggestions may be found wanting, and there are certainly other good ideas out there. The keys to a stronger future for Illinois lie in planning, fiscal stability and predictability, discipline, constraint, investment where necessary, and adoption of policies that build on the state's many strengths.

We want to be—and we can be—proud of our state again.

CHAPTER 1

The Changing Faces of Illinois

The late North Carolina governor Terry Sanford once lamented that there is no one in the governor's office whose only job is to gaze out the window and brood about the problems of the future.[1] So it is in Illinois. Unfortunately, Illinois doesn't know where it is going. There is no planning agency within state government to chart a course for the coming five to ten years. There are no privately supported grand plans for the state such as Daniel Burnham's 1909 plan for Chicago, with its wide boulevards, great parks, and a lakefront protected for the citizenry. The Chicago Metropolitan Agency for Planning (CMAP) has produced a comprehensive plan for the region called *Go to 2040*.[2] This plan encompasses much of the population of Illinois yet leaves out most of the geography of the state and focuses largely on local government issues.

Instead of long-term planning, Illinois simply carries on year by year. State government struggles to pay its long-overdue bills from previous years and craft a budget that will not worsen the state's deficit situation. State lawmakers process thousands of legislative proposals each year, which in totality may represent the closest thing to a plan for Illinois.

This book looks back on where Illinois has been in recent decades, assesses where things stand as of this writing, and tries to project where the state is heading, based on trends of the past few decades. The book also lays out numbered suggestions and recommendations for the future, proposals that might change the state's trajectory for the better.

In this chapter we provide a backdrop for the rest of the book by examining demographic, economic, and social change in Illinois. We also gauge the public's mood and the state's strengths. In subsequent chapters we evaluate the major components of our state and its local governments, with an eye to public policy suggestions for the future that might appeal to readers, or might not, and of the potential improvements the options might bring the state.

A Brief Historical Overview

The "Tall State," as it was called in a early tourism campaign, stretches almost four hundred miles from the Wisconsin line to its southern tip at Cairo (pronounced "kay'-ro"), nestled between Kentucky and Missouri. The northernmost latitude is on line with Portsmouth, New Hampshire, and at Cairo, close to that of Portsmouth, Virginia.[3]

The state's diversity is due in great measure to U.S. territorial delegate Nathaniel Pope, who in 1818 succeeded in passing an amendment to the Illinois Enabling Act that moved the new state's northern boundary forty-one miles to the north of the original plan. This addition of eight thousand square miles—mostly wilderness at the time—today encompasses metropolitan Chicago and about two-thirds of the state's population; without it, Illinois would have voted Democratic in 1860 and Abraham Lincoln could not have been elected president.[4]

Because it was settled originally by southerners, there was pro-slavery sentiment among many in 1818. Three of the first four governors possessed registered servants, "a theoretical distinction with slavery that made little difference to the Negroes involved."[5] A white man could import blacks under fifteen years of age and register them to serve until they were in their thirties. A black person had the right to reject a registered servant contract, in which case the owner could return him to a southern state within sixty days.[6]

Settlement of the state was facilitated by natural factors, ingenuity, and human achievements. The Ohio River offered a convenient super-waterway, while the state's generally level topography made the tall-grass prairie relatively easy to traverse on foot. Opening of the Erie Canal in New York in 1825 facilitated the flow of Yankees and European immigrants via the Great Lakes. The early development of Illinois as a railroad center helped disperse throughout the state those newly arrived; later, the main line of the Illinois Central Railroad, running from New Orleans, would bring tens of thousands of blacks to jobs in Chicago.

The platting, or dividing, of Illinois into townships of thirty-six uniform one-mile squares, as decreed by the U.S. Congress in the Northwest Ordinances of 1785 and 1787, was designed to transfer public lands efficiently into private hands.[7] This it did. Each mile square represented a "section" of land of 640 acres. Township roads were laid out along the sections. The township plats made it simple to survey and sell virgin land with a minimum of confusion and dispute. Even today, for the airplane traveler crossing Illinois, a geometric checkerboard pattern unfolds below.

There was a hunger to develop this rich flatland, but transportation infrastructure was needed first in order to get the settlers in and the bounty of the fields to market. When Abraham Lincoln and Stephen A. Douglas served as state lawmakers in the 1830s, the legislature embarked on an ambitious scheme of "internal improvements," but the dreamed-of network of wood-plank roads, canals, and railroads collapsed under the weight of poor planning, a weak national economy, and a lack of both capital and engineering capacity.[8] Lincoln and Douglas later became U.S. congressmen and revived the idea, this time convincing the federal government to assist with huge land grants for private investors. In 1851 the federal government offered 3.75 million acres of railroad right-of-way and adjoining land to investors in the Illinois Central Railroad (IC). Within five years, 705 miles of track had been laid from Cairo to Galena, with a spur to Chicago. The IC became the longest railway in the world and the nation's largest private venture to date.

Railroads served as the interstate highways of the nineteenth century. If a town was on a rail line, it generally prospered; if not, the town was often abandoned. Railroad trackage in Illinois increased from 111 miles in 1850 to 2,800 in 1860 and 7,000 by 1875. In part because of its railroad grid, Illinois was the fastest-growing territory in the world by the middle of the nineteenth century.[9] The thirty-six million acres of land in Illinois were enough for almost a quarter-million quarter-section (160-acre) farms. One-fourth of those farms had been taken by 1850, and nearly all by 1875. Three in four farms were within five miles of a railroad, and only 5 percent were more than ten miles distant.[10]

Early Triumph for the "Modernizers"

In the free-for-all environment of the state's early days, no one culture held sway. This northern state had been settled first by southerners, primarily poor, land-hungry northern British and Scots-Irish pioneers from the uplands of Virginia and the Carolinas, up through Tennessee and Kentucky.[11] James Simeone describes the first settlers as the "white folks" who saw the West (Illinois Territory) as a place of opportunity and feared the re-establishment of an economic aristocracy by English and old Virginia families.[12]

The second surge came in the 1830s via the new Erie Canal, primarily from New England and the Middle Atlantic states. These Yankees, most of whom settled in the central and northern parts of Illinois, generally brought more assets with them and put down roots into richer farmland than did those farther south.

These demographics set the stage for a struggle between the "white folks" in southern Illinois and the "modernizers," primarily Yankees, in the north.[13] The genius of the modernizers, according to Richard Jensen, lay in a combination of values: faith in reason, a drive for middle-class status, equal rights, and a sense of mission to transform the world in their image. Education was their remedy, efficiency their ideal.

Everyone in Illinois recognized the difference between modernizers and white folks, or "traditionalists," as Richard Jensen identified them, although nobody used those words. Each group thought the other peculiar. Fast-talking Yankee peddlers were distrusted—one county even set a prohibitive fifty-dollars-per-quarter license for clock peddlers. A Yankee woman was amused by the drinking, horse trading, and quaint, slow drawl of the southerners. She talked with one who allowed that "it's a right smart thing to be able to read when you want to" but who didn't figure that books and the sciences would "do a man as much good as handy use of the rifle."[14]

Strong commitment to education was the hallmark of the modernizers. By 1883 the northern part of the state provided its children with one-third more days of schooling than did the schools in "Egypt," as deep southern Illinois, with its towns of Cairo, Karnak, and Thebes, was called.[15] Jensen quotes a nineteenth-century governor on the values in northern Illinois: "Is a school house, a bridge, or a church to be built, a road to be made, a school or minister to be maintained, or taxes to be paid? The northern man is never to be found wanting."[16]

By 1860 the Yankee modernizers dominated northern Illinois politics, while traditionalists held sway in the south. Central Illinois became the uncertain political battleground. With Lincoln's election and the ensuing Civil War, the modernists triumphed and, through the Republican Party, controlled Illinois politics almost continuously for the following seventy years. (In order to emphasize that generalizations about traditionalists and modernizers are just that, we note that Lincoln the modernizer came from traditionalist Kentucky roots while Douglas, who represented the traditionalist viewpoint in the 1860 presidential election, came from upstate New York.)

Chicago and the Great Midwest

Another cultural characteristic that emerged in the nineteenth century, with roots in commerce, would mark Illinois forever. In a compelling synthesis of the organic relationship between a great city and the vast prairie that envelops it, William Cronon explains that neither Chicago nor the rich countryside of the Midwest would have developed their great wealth if not for the symbiosis between the two: the urban center contributing creativity, energy, and capital while the farmers and small towns provided ambition, intelligence, and the harvest from incredibly fecund soils.[17] Plentiful water and easy waterborne transportation provided further economic stimulus. The Wabash, Ohio, and Mississippi Rivers formed Illinois's natural boundaries and the Illinois River traversed the middle, positioning the state to be at the heart of the young nation's economic expansion.[18]

At the southern tip of Lake Michigan, Chicago sat astride the boundary between East and West. Chicago's meatpackers, grain merchants, and manufacturers showed extraordinary drive and creativity, not to mention a knack for attracting capital. The railroads were eager to carry their goods, and these capitalists put the Midwest's natural resources to use to create an unprecedented hive of economic development by the end of the 1800s.

Almost all the Chicago capitalists were Yankees such as meatpackers Philip Swift and Gustavus Armour. These two men and their collaborators systematized the market in animal flesh. Building on the adage that "the hog is regarded as the most compact form in which the Indian corn crop . . . can be transported to market," they created hog slaughtering lines that were the forerunners of the assembly line.[19] Cattle were standardized as Grade No. 1, No. 2, or No. 3. Rail cars were refrigerated so that dressed beef from Chicago could be marketed in the East.

According to Cronon, the overarching genius of Swift and Armour lay in the immense impersonal, hierarchical organizations they created, operated by an army of managers and workers who would outlive and carry on after the founders. By 1880 Chicago had more than seventy-five thousand industrial workers, the largest such labor force west of the Appalachians.[20] To quote muckraker Frank Norris: "The Great Grey City, brooking no rival, imposed its dominion upon a reach of country larger than many a kingdom of the Old World."[21]

By 1890 Chicago, with more than a million residents, was the nation's second-largest city. It bragged on itself in 1893 by presenting the World's Columbian Exposition to twenty-seven million visitors. From a one-square-mile tract of marshes and scrub pines on the south side of Chicago arose a fairy city that hosted the exhibits of forty-six nations, a single exposition building said to seat three hundred thousand persons, and an amusement park ride by George Ferris of Downstate Galesburg that could carry forty persons in each of thirty-six cars on a 250-foot-high revolving wheel.[22] Visitors were equally impressed with the real-world development a few miles up the lakefront in the city center. At twenty-one stories, the Masonic Temple was the world's tallest building, a so-called skyscraper.

There was a tension between the fairy city of the exposition and the real city that surrounded it, a tension that persists to this day. Rural visitors from Downstate were agog at the artificial White City but "afeared" of the perceived dangers and tumult of Chicago. Many Chicagoans, in fact, had already become eager for the tranquility of the country. In 1868 the urban planner Frederick Law Olmsted designed Riverside, west of Chicago, as a new community where families could enjoy the country while the breadwinner could take the train to his job downtown. Skyscraper and suburb created each other, said Cronon, and the railroad made both possible.[23]

By 1930 Chicago had a population of 3.4 million inhabitants—almost half the state's total—and was the fourth-largest city in the world, second only to New York in the United States. By 1945 Chicago peaked at 3.6 million, as the suburban era began in earnest. Auto ownership doubled between 1945 and the early 1950s, and expressways were being built, foreshadowing suburban growth. According to the historian Jensen, "Comfort, security, and the promise of continued progress . . . made the suburban era a time of placid complacency."[24]

With Chicago leading the way and many Downstate communities still thriving under mixed industrial and agricultural economies, Illinois was a strong state through most of the twentieth century. But driven as it was by commercial success and with a line of local and statewide leaders who worked closely with and profited from business interests, Chicago became a place where the wealth of opportunity was matched only by the ruthlessness of those pursuing it.

The writer Nelson Algren, in his prose poem "Chicago: City on the Make," identified two key characteristics of the culture that came to dominate Illinois. First, leadership and success were highly prized, and second, if the success involved a bit of shady dealing, so be it. "If he can get away with it I give the man credit," Algren said of a safe-blower. The same culture has always looked askance at weakness, having no sympathy for a woman reduced to prostitution or a jobless man numbing himself with beer. Warned Algren: "Wise up,

Jim: it's a joint where the bulls and the foxes live well and the lambs wind up head-down from the hook."[25]

The Chicago business leader Paul O'Connor put it in more positive vein:

> We [Chicago] invented the skyscraper, split the atom, made our river flow backwards, created a lakefront from scratch, figured out the transistor, drew all the railroads to us, pioneered and continuously dominated commercial air travel, broadcast the world's first all-color TV station, built the number-one manufacturing city of America, invented risk management markets, won more Nobel Prizes than any city on earth, communicate[d] more data on a daily basis than any other city on earth, threw away more basic industries than most other cities ever had, you know, like, hog butcher, stacker of wheat, steel capital of America. Should we tell anyone?[26]

Regionalism and a Lack of Sense of Statehood

Illinois has been characterized throughout by perceptions among its citizens that the state is divided into geopolitical regions, each of which looks after its own interests through state government. Before the Civil War, Democrats in the south of the state and Republicans in the north clashed over the extension of slavery. After the war, with the rapid growth of Chicago and its large foreign-born population, the city and the rest of Illinois saw their interests divide along urban-rural as well as Democratic (Chicago) and Republican (Downstate) lines.

With the explosive growth of the suburbs around Chicago following World War II, the suburban counties that formed a collar around Chicago became a third regional force. A state constitutional amendment of 1954 formalized this tripartite sectionalism in redistricting.[27] Legislative district lines were to be drawn exclusively within Chicago, the suburban collar, or Downstate; the amendment has since been superseded by U.S. Supreme Court decisions concerning redistricting. Today, the three regions differ with regard to transportation, environmental, gun ownership, and social issues, as well as over the allocation of the state budget.

Possibly as a result of this regionalism, Illinois and its residents lack a sense of statehood of the sort you find in Texas. There is in Illinois no "The Eyes of Texas Are upon You" to rally citizens around the state flag. When traveling, few state residents identify themselves as from Illinois; instead, they are from Chicago, "near Chicago," and maybe "southern Illinois."

Nor is there much intercourse among the regions that would familiarize one with the other. Chicago-area residents tend to vacation in Wisconsin or Michigan rather than Downstate. Downstaters may go to Cubs or Bears games in Chicago, yet they don't stray far from their cars or buses after the game. Suburbanites may go to work in Chicago, yet many others rarely go into the city. And southern Illinois residents are closer to Oxford, Mississippi, than they are to Chicago. So there is little to bind residents across the state into a force for Illinois *as* Illinois.

The state is also fragmented by its multitudinous local governments. It has more than six thousand separate taxing units, more than any state in the nation. In addition to 284 municipalities, the metropolitan Chicago region encompasses in total more than 1,226 local governments. By contrast, the New York metropolitan area has fewer than 200.[28]

Is Demography Destiny?

The state's population has been growing more slowly than that of the nation. In the period 2000–2010, Illinois's population grew by 3.3 percent, while that of the nation grew by almost 10 percent, reflecting a pattern of relatively slow growth in Illinois that goes back to 1970.[29] There has also been a dramatic change in the mix of people who live in Illinois.

Since about 1970, Illinois has been exporting residents to other states, primarily to the South and the Southwest, while the state has been importing residents from other countries, primarily from Latin America and from Asia. We estimate that between 1970 and the present, two million more whites have left the state than have migrated to the state.[30] During the same period there has been an influx of Latinos and Asians. In 1970, minorities represented just 11.9 percent of the Illinois population whereas as of 2010 the proportion of minorities had reached 34.9 percent (black, 14.5 percent; Latino, 15.8, and Asian, 4.6).[31] In 1980 whites represented 78 percent of the Illinois population, or 8.91 million, whereas in 2010 that percentage had shrunk to 63.7 percent, or 8.17 million persons. In the same period, the number of Latinos in Illinois grew from 636,000 to 2 million.

Between 2000 and 2010 Illinois would have lost population had it not been for the increase in the Latino population by 497,000, most of which was caused by births among families already in Illinois. Half of all students enrolled in Illinois public schools now come from minority groups.[32]

Rural Illinois and Chicago have been losing population for decades, though Chicago's population rose by about 10,000 between July 2011 and July 2012, making it the slowest-growing major U.S. city, according to the Associated Press.[33] At the end of World War II, Chicago had 3.5 million people and as of 2010 it had 2.7 million. Much of western and southern Illinois has been losing population since 1880, when nearly every 160-acre quarter-section of land had a farm residence, to today, when a single farm family may till two to three thousand acres or more. Rural Illinois lost 12 percent of residents up to age forty-four between 2000 and 2010, while rural areas of our neighboring states were losing only about 6 percent.[34] The suburban collar around Chicago, basically a postwar phenomenon, now represents 5.9 million residents, or 46 percent of the state's population.

There are also bulges and dips on the age timeline. Between 2000 and 2010 there was a 25 percent increase in the baby boom generation (ages forty-five to sixty-four). According to the sociologist Matthew Hall, "This movement up the population pyramid—something demographers colloquially refer to as a pig moving through a python—has potentially profound effects for policymakers."[35] That this group is at the peak of its earning power should provide a bonus for tax receipts in the period 2015–25. However, as those above the age of sixty move into retirement and are replaced by smaller numbers of residents coming along after the baby boom, tax receipts will probably suffer.

A Slow-Growing Economy

The Illinois economy has also been growing slowly relative to the U.S. economy and even more slowly than the rest of the Midwest (see figure 1). In 1948 the state's average per capita income was 128 percent of the national average of 100 percent; over the decades, that figure declined to 105 percent of the national average in 2011.[36] The state is still wealthier than the national average, but much less so than it was right after World War II. In the first decade of the twenty-first century, Illinois ranked forty-seventh among the states in real gross state product growth.[37] According to Frank Beal of Metropolis Strategies, a Chicago think tank, the Chicagoland regional economy has lost momentum during the decade. Not only did the gross product of the Chicago region decline relative to the nation's during this period, but the region's average annual growth in gross product, at 3 percent from 2000 to 2010, ranked fourteenth among the fifteen top metropolitan economies in the United States.[38]

Job losses in Illinois were particularly heavy during the same time frame. Geoffrey Hewings of the Regional Economics Applications Laboratory at the University of Illinois notes that from the employment peak of November 2000, Illinois lost 655,700 jobs and had regained only 192,000 of those jobs by March 2013.[39]

Rural Illinois lags behind the metropolitan areas. Median household income varies dramatically by county across the state, with the highest median incomes in the collar counties around Chicago and the lowest incomes

FIGURE 1. Total nonfarm employment growth rate, January 1990–March 2013

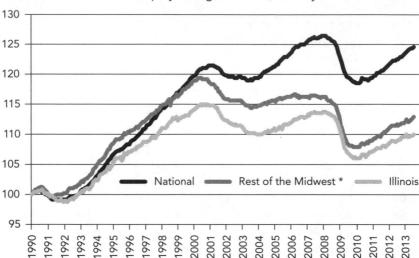

Note: *Rest of the Midwest = Indiana, Iowa, Michigan, Missouri, Ohio, and Wisconsin
Source: Illinois Jobs Index, Regional Economics Analysis Laboratory (www.real.illinois
.edu), University of Illinois, April 30, 2013.

in southern and western Illinois. In 2011, for example, Lake and McHenry Counties in the suburban collar registered median household incomes of $79,666 and $76,909, respectively. In contrast, at the southern tip of Illinois, Alexander County reported only $27,727, less than half of the median state-wide household income of $56,576, and Hardin and Pulaski Counties, also in southern Illinois, reported about $31,000 each.[40]

We believe this wide gap in countywide household incomes can be explained in part by what we call the "Tale of Two Families," which is based on real-life illustrations from Nowlan's home area of western Illinois (see table 1). The dynamic results from the interplay of the facts that more women have begun working during the past generation and that all fields of professional work are now open to women. This is combined with the reality that like kinds marry.

The illustration of the Smith and Jones families represents, to the extent we can generalize from it, a national phenomenon. Within Illinois, we believe the illustration contributes to what we might call a "Tale of Two States," one in the suburbs that is generally well-educated and prosperous, another largely Downstate, as well as in big parts of Chicago and the inner suburbs, that is poorly educated and falling behind economically.

TABLE 1. Illustration of family income ratios, 1970 and 2012

1970	Income
Smith Family	
John works at Harvester Works @ $25 per hour × 2,000 hours	$50,000
Wife Molly at home with the children	
Jones Family	
Dr. David Jones, MD, in private practice	$150,000
Wife Polly, RN, at home	
1970 ratio of Jones family income to Smith family income	**3/1**

2012	Income
Smith Family	
John Smith Jr. works at slaughtering plant, 40 hours @ $10 per hour	$20,000
Young Molly works at WalMart @ $8 per hour × 2,000 hours	$16,000
Total income	$36,000
Jones Family	
Dr. David Jones Jr., MD, in private practice	$225,000
Dr. Mary Jones, MD, in private practice	$225,000
Total income	$450,000
2012 ratio of Jones family income to Smith family income	**13/1**

Source: Provided by the authors. All figures approximate and in current dollars.

Illinois Residents in a Funk

When the authors were boys growing up in Illinois in the 1950s, Illinois was a proud, positive state, one of the wealthiest in the nation, vibrant and growing. Not today. The people of Illinois seem to be in a depressed state of mind, or a slump, based on the overall tone of the responses to a 2011 newspaper column by Jim Nowlan about the future of Illinois.[41] We present excerpts from readers' replies below, with limited identifying information.

For example, in response to the column, one reader, Robin, felt that "we are headed in the wrong direction," largely because of the recent tax increase and the high costs of doing business in Illinois.

Robin and his wife have resided in Illinois for twenty-seven years, but they "have had enough" and are seriously considering moving out of state. Robin used the contrast between Iowa (nonpartisan redistricting) and Illinois (political gerrymandering) as an illustration of what he doesn't like about our state.

The small, unscientific sample of responses comes down hard on the culture of corruption as one of the biggest problems for Illinois. "I am sure the political climate in Iowa is much the same as Illinois," Robin noted, "but at least we could rid ourselves of the rotten smell of political corruption that seems to hover over this state like a foul odor."

Chuck agreed: "I am pessimistic when I see people's indifference to the rampant, destructive corruption in the state. . . . If people aren't outraged about the illegal 'Big C' corruption then there is little chance of rooting out the legal but morally deficient 'small c' influence peddling and vote buying parasites that sap the energy of the state."

Georgene added: "In the past few years it has become an embarrassment to admit that I live here. I believe the state is corrupted beyond repair and our so-called leaders are a national joke that is not funny." Charles mused, "The people of Illinois seem to take a perverse pride in being known as one of the most corrupt states in the nation."

Clearly, residents of Illinois feel something is wrong. For example, the annual Illinois Policy Survey by Northern Illinois University found in 2011 that 68 percent of those surveyed were "not satisfied" with the way things are going and only 12 percent were satisfied.[42] This represents a dramatic increase in those not satisfied from 1998, when only 10 percent were not satisfied and 51 percent were satisfied. Similarly, a 2010 poll by the Paul Simon Institute at Southern Illinois University found that "almost eight in ten thought things were off track and headed in the wrong direction" in the state.[43]

And much of the blame is focused on our state government. A survey of southern Illinois residents in 2011 found that 59 percent felt that state government had a "mostly harmful" effect on daily life.[44] A statewide survey done for the Joyce Foundation in 2009 found that 81 percent trust state government only "some of the time" (52 percent) or "almost never" (29 percent).[45]

Nor are we liked much by outsiders. A 2012 survey by Public Policy Polling found that Illinois was the second most disliked state in the nation after California.[46] While Americans generally have a favorable view of most states, five received net unfavorable ratings from Americans surveyed, led by California (27 percent favorable view and 44 unfavorable) followed by Illinois (19 percent to 29 percent, with 52 percent having no opinion). Hawaii was viewed most favorably, 54 percent to 10 percent, followed by Colorado (44 percent to 9 percent).

State Government Changing, Growing

Illinois state government has changed dramatically since 1970. For example, there is a much larger prisoner population to support: in 1970 there were eight thousand inmates in our state's prisons; by 2013 the number had increased more than sixfold, to forty-nine thousand. The number of residents covered by Medicaid, the federal-state program of health care for low-income people, children, and many middle-class residents in nursing homes, had grown from six hundred thousand in 1970 to 2.7 million in 2013. On the other hand, the number of persons covered by the program called Temporary Assistance to Needy Families declined from 923,000 in 1984 (when it was called Aid to Families with Dependent Children) to fewer than 47,000 families (the Department of Human Services now counts families rather than individuals) in 2011.[47]

In order to accommodate these changes in the level of state government services, especially for Medicaid, in which the state bears about 45 percent of the cost, and for public pension system obligations, spending has increased. This increase, however, has been faster than the rate of inflation. In 1978, Illinois state government appropriated $10.7 billion from all funds, which would be $37.2 billion in 2012 dollars, adjusted for inflation. In fact, fiscal year (FY) 2012 appropriations were $60 billion, or 62 percent more than $37.2 billion.[48] In the same period, the individual income tax rate has doubled from 2.5 percent to a temporary rate of 5 percent.

Illinois Has a Lot Going for It

When we asked economic development professionals to identify Illinois's selling points, they responded with location, transportation infrastructure, and workforce. Being in the middle of the nation is a big plus. The state is also arguably the transportation hub of the nation.[49] For example, Chicago is the only city served by the six largest North American railroads. Every day, five hundred freight trains pass through the city. The Chicago region is also the third-busiest container-moving port in the world, behind only Hong Kong and Singapore. And Illinois's airport system is not only the second-largest in the nation but also the best-connected to the nation and the world of any American airport as of 2013.[50] In terms of the percentage of its adult population with bachelor's degrees or more, Illinois ranks thirteenth among the states, with 31 percent.[51]

We would add that Chicago represents a strong plus for its state, especially in the global age. In 2010, *Foreign Policy* magazine ranked Chicago the sixth "most global city" in the world, based on twenty-five metrics across five dimensions, behind only New York in the United States. And in 2013, the respected Economist Intelligence Unit projected that Chicago will rank ninth among the world's top 120 global cities in 2025 in its ability to attract capital, talent, businesses, and people, joining New York as the only two U.S. cities in the top 10 worldwide.[52]

In the chapters that follow we lay out suggestions and recommendations, in a context of tight state budgets, that we feel might be beneficial for the state and that we hope might bend the state's slow growth curve in a more positive direction.

CHAPTER 2

Fixing Past Budgeting Sins

Persistent annual state budget deficits in the early twenty-first century and huge unfunded liabilities in our state pension systems have made Illinois a symbol of dereliction of fiscal responsibilities. That is why we make budgeting the first substantive chapter of this book. This chapter provides an overview of our fiscal system, discusses the major causes of the deficits the state has been sustaining, and provides suggestions for managing our resources more effectively, revamping our revenue system and balancing our state budget.

Illinois has a rather typical state and local government revenue system. That is, the state imposes taxes on income and sales, and local governments impose a tax on property valuation, and state and local governments have established myriad other taxes and fees. In 2012, Illinois state government imposed twenty-six taxes and collected 1,504 separate fees.[1] As can be seen in figures 2 and 3, in 2012 the state took in revenues of $64.5 billion and spent $67.9 billion.[2] The individual income tax is the largest source of state revenue, at $17 billion. The property tax is in Illinois, and in most states, solely a local government revenue source. Not shown in figure 2 is the $26 billion generated locally in 2011 by the property tax for our state's 6,020 local taxing units. Because state revenues and the local property tax are both utilized for school funding, a decrease in state revenues that results from, say, reducing taxes often results in increases in local property taxes.

In 2011 the flat-rate individual income tax in Illinois was increased from 3 percent to 5 percent, and the rate of the corporate income tax from 7.3

FIGURE 2. FY2012 state government revenues, excluding borrowing
($ in millions); total: $64,514

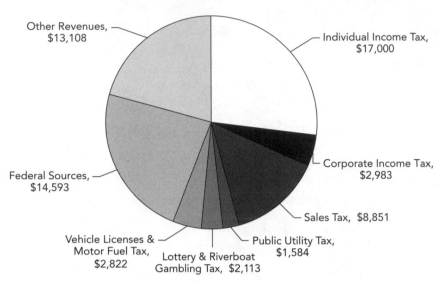

Other Revenues, $13,108

Individual Income Tax, $17,000

Federal Sources, $14,593

Corporate Income Tax, $2,983

Sales Tax, $8,851

Vehicle Licenses & Motor Fuel Tax, $2,822

Lottery & Riverboat Gambling Tax, $2,113

Public Utility Tax, $1,584

Source: Traditional Budgetary Financial Report, Illinois Office of the Comptroller, 2013.

percent to 9.5 percent. The rates are temporary and are to begin a stair-step of reductions beginning January 1, 2015. It is not surprising that the significant rate increases of 2011 have raised the overall percentage of the state's economic activity devoted to state and local taxes to 9.53 percent of gross domestic product in 2011, above the national average of 8.95 percent. This increased Illinois's ranking among the states from twenty-ninth highest in 2009 to fifteenth highest in 2011.[3] The Illinois revenue mix is typical, but not all states are typical. For example, neither Florida nor Texas, competitors of Illinois for economic development, has an income tax. Those states do benefit from heavy tourism and petroleum resources, respectively, yet the fact remains that Illinois policymakers should keep states such as these as well as neighboring states in mind when setting revenue policy for our state.

Spending for health care and human services in FY2012 represented 37 percent of state spending, while that for all education was just 22 percent (see figure 3).[4] The federal-state Medicaid program, which provides health care for low-income residents, alone accounts for more dollars than the state expends on education. In 1991 Medicaid accounted for less than half the amount the state spent on education.[5] But persistent high rates of increase in healthcare spending since then, much steeper than the increase in the rate of inflation,

FIGURE 3. FY2012 state spending ($ in millions); total: $67,873

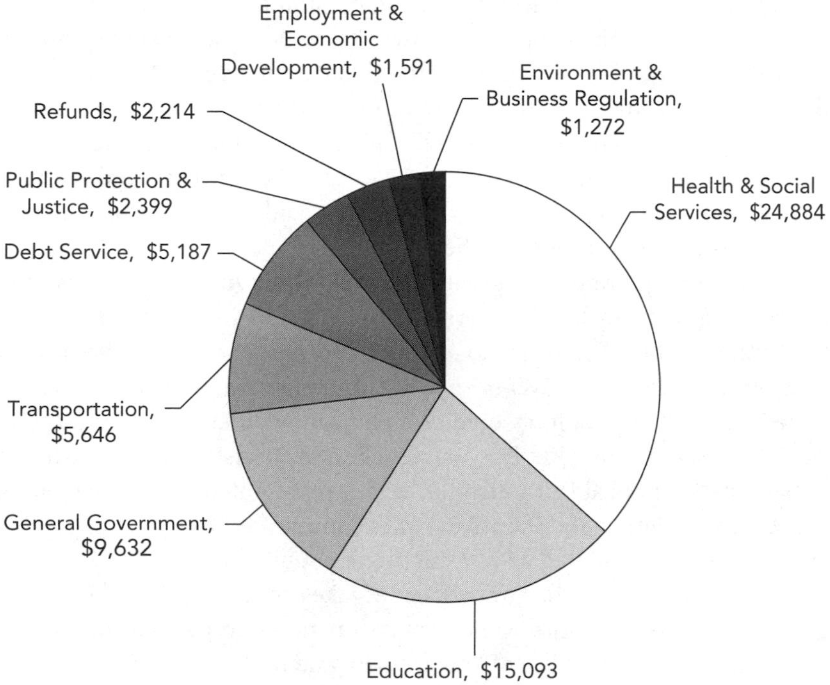

Employment &
Economic
Development, $1,591

Environment &
Business Regulation,
$1,272

Refunds, $2,214

Public Protection &
Justice, $2,399

Health & Social
Services, $24,884

Debt Service, $5,187

Transportation,
$5,646

General Government,
$9,632

Education, $15,093

Source: Traditional Budgetary Financial Report, Illinois Office of the Comptroller, 2013.

have forced a shift in the allocation of state dollars from education to health care. Over recent decades there has also been a sharp increase in spending for corrections, which now amounts to $1.3 billion.

Spending for "General Government" in FY2012, which basically means support for the operations of state government, represented just 14 percent of total state spending. Indeed, most state spending is distributed in the form of support to local governments such as local public school districts, municipalities, and counties and to healthcare or human service providers, usually not-for-profit organizations.

Crafting the Annual Illinois Budget

The state budget is the annual plan for spending from available resources. Budgets take in revenues and redistribute them through spending programs, generally from richer persons and regions to poorer ones. In 1989 the Illinois

Legislative Research Unit conducted a limited analysis of where tax revenue came from in Illinois, by geopolitical region, and of where those revenues were distributed.[6] The report found that the region comprising suburban Cook County (outside Chicago) and the collar counties paid 46.4 percent of the major taxes analyzed and received 27.4 percent of the distributions for such programs as school aid and highway projects. Downstate Illinois (the 96 counties outside the "collar") paid 32.9 percent of the taxes and received 47.1 percent of the program resources. Chicago paid 20.7 percent of the taxes and received 25.4 percent of the benefits.

These findings are not surprising, because Downstate Illinois was (and is today) significantly less prosperous on a per capita income basis than are the collar counties. The study nonetheless became controversial because of what it revealed and has never been updated and refined. There is little reason to believe that the situation would be significantly different if conducted in 2014. For example, in 2009 Downstate school districts received 50 percent of basic state school aid although the region represented only 35 percent of the state's population; the suburban collar counties received only 18 percent although they represented 24 percent of the population.[7]

About a year before the annual budget takes effect on July 1, the Illinois government's sixty or more agencies make financial requests for the coming year to the Governor's Office of Management and Budget (GOMB), based on guidelines that it provided to the agencies earlier. That office reviews requests and makes decisions in the fall as to how much each agency will be allocated in the annual budget. Then GOMB forwards its total proposed spending plan to the governor for his review and amendment.[8]

In the new year, the governor presents his spending plan to the Illinois General Assembly. In the spring, the lawmakers hold hearings on the governor's proposal and make changes in his plan, which they enact and send back to the governor for his response. In the summer, the governor may veto the whole budget bill or veto specific line items in the bill as well as reduce other specific lines. The lawmakers then have an opportunity in the fall to override the governor's veto actions. The process is summarized in the following table.

Summer	Fall	December	Spring	Summer	Fall
Agencies >	GOMB >	Governor >	Legislature >	Governor >	Legislature

Budgeting is really simple: (1) start with the amount of money in the bank at the end of a year; (2) estimate your receipts for the coming year; (3) decide what you want to have in the bank at the end of the budget period; (4) subtract item 3 from the sum of the first two items; (5) allocate the remaining amount among programs. "That's all there is to it. That's the truth," says Robert Mandeville, director of the state budget office from 1977 to 1990.[9] Simple, maybe, but never easy, because of step number 5.

How Did We Get into This Mess?

Since 2000, Illinois state government has been spending more—a lot more— than it has been generating in revenues. "How can that be?" a person asks, as the Illinois Constitution requires a balanced budget. Yes, but borrowed funds fall into the constitutional characterization of funds available. The fact that it creates a debt for a future year does not mean that the state has failed to meet the requirement of a balanced budget in the year the funds were borrowed. Figure 4 shows that between 2002 and 2011 (the latest year for which data are available) State of Illinois net assets declined from –$5.7 billion to –$42.5 billion, or about $4 billion per year, primarily because of spending and obligating more than the state was receiving in revenues. And during this period, the state also either borrowed to make annual pension payments or failed to make adequate payments. As a result, the annual average overspending and under-obligating amounted to about $7 billion. This is about the same amount that is being generated by the temporary income tax increases of 2011, when the individual income tax rate was increased from 3 percent to 5 percent and the corporate income tax was raised to 9.5 percent.

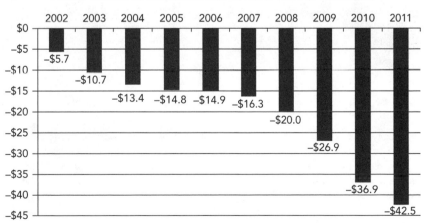

FIGURE 4. State of Illinois net assets, 2002–2011 ($ in billions)

Source: Comprehensive Annual Financial Reports, Illinois Office of the Comptroller, Springfield, various years.

So, even with the tax increases, the new revenues appear to be inadequate to balance the budget and also pay off about $8 billion in outstanding bills to vendors, at least not based on historic spending patterns. And because Illinois is often months late in paying its bills, former state budget director David Vaught estimates that the state pays 6–10 percent more to vendors than it would otherwise because the vendors must often borrow while waiting to be paid.[10]

The Fiscal Futures Model of the Illinois budget, maintained by the University of Illinois Institute of Government and Public Affairs, shows that if the higher income tax rates are *retained* past the 2015 beginning expiration date, the annual budget deficit would be substantially reduced, but not eliminated (see figure 5.)[11] If, on the other hand, the income tax rates are *reduced* in 2015 as called for by statute, the Fiscal Futures Model projects that the backlog of unpaid bills is expected to grow to more than $20 billion in FY2018 from about $8 billion in FY2013.[12]

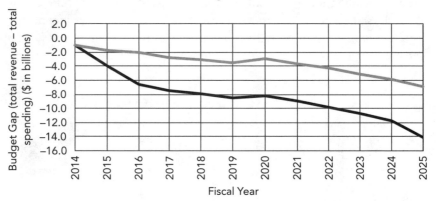

FIGURE 5. Illinois consolidated funds budget gap projections to FY2025, with and without phaseout of higher income tax rates after 2014

Notes: (1) Revenue and spending figures are from over seven hundred state funds, not just the four General Funds. (2) In order to highlight *sustainable revenues*, new borrowing and decreases in preexisting fund balances are not counted as revenue. (3) These are *annual* budget gap projections, which add up over time. Also, no adjustment is made for how funding one year's deficit might affect revenue or spending in the next year.

Source: IGPA Fiscal Futures Model, October 2013 (thus before any savings from December 2013 pension reform). See http://igpa.uillinois.edu/system/files/Fiscal-Futures-Projections-Oct-2013.pdf.

There are three phenomena that apply in Illinois budgeting. First, elected officials, many of whom are career politicos, like to do things *for* their voters, such as increased spending for human services programs, and they resist doing things *to* their voters, such as increase taxes. This creates a bias toward spending more than the revenues being generated.

Second, Illinois has what economists call a "structural deficit," that is, annual spending increases for such programs as health care and social services grow at a rate higher than the rate of increase in revenues.[13] Using the Fiscal Futures Model, Richard Dye and his associates at the University of Illinois predict that revenues will grow more slowly than expenditures in the future. They predict that state spending is projected to grow in coming years at 3.7 percent per year while revenue is expected to grow at 2.3 percent.[14]

Third, citizens oppose cuts in spending for most state government programs. A 2012 survey by the Paul Simon Public Policy Institute found that strong majorities opposed cuts in spending for literally all categories of spending, from education (80 percent opposed) to public safety (73.8 percent) to people with disabilities (83.5 percent).[15] (See table 2.) These three phenomena have contributed to the deep financial hole into which Illinois has descended.

Throughout the period 2001–12, Illinois budgets employed cardinal sins of public finance: borrowing for operations and selling long-term assets for short-term operating expenditures. In 2011, for example, Illinois sold its long-term payments from the tobacco industry (which had been going into a "Tobacco [Lawsuit] Settlement Fund") for $1.5 billion, which the state promptly spent to try to balance its operating budget for that year. During the decade, the legislature and the governor borrowed $17.2 billion for long-term pen-

TABLE 2. Public support in Illinois for budget cutting, 2011

Do you favor or oppose cuts in spending for:	Favor	Oppose
K–12 education	16.5%	80.0%
State universities	38.2	54.1
State police and prisons	20.6	73.8
Parks and environment	36.7	55.6
Programs for poor people	25.2	64.7
People with mental and physical disabilities	12.3	83.5
Pension benefits for state employees	45.5	48.0

Source: Charles Leonard, Ryan P. Burge, and Emily S. Carroll, "The Movement of Opinion Toward Spending Cuts," The Simon Review, Paper no. 27, Paul Simon Public Policy Institute, Southern Illinois University, Carbondale, January 2012, p. 32.

sion obligation purposes but used part of the proceeds from the bonds to fill gaps in the annual operating budgets. Further, the state policymakers delayed payments to vendors.[16]

So we understand how borrowed funds can offset a budget deficit, but how do we get ourselves into the situation of not paying vendors' bills in a balanced budget environment? Section 25 of the State Finance Act provides that expenditure of funds for liabilities incurred within a given fiscal year must be paid from that year's appropriations, *with certain exceptions*. The two major exceptions are for liabilities associated with Medicaid and with employee and retiree health insurance, two relatively large areas of annual spending. Current-year liabilities can be paid out of future years' appropriations. So if we don't appropriate enough funds to pay all of the bills associated with these exceptions in a given year, the budget may appear balanced, but future year's appropriations will be required to pay current-year liabilities. The governor has estimated that the Section 25 exceptions will amount to almost $3.2 billion at the end of FY2013. One of the Medicaid reforms enacted in 2012 was to limit the amount of Section 25 exceptions attributable to Medicaid expenditures authorized in future fiscal years, but it does not limit the amount of expenditures for all Section 25 exceptions.

1. Require that all expenditures of funds for liabilities incurred in a given year be paid from appropriations for that year only.

Pension Underfunding: Effects on Future Budgets

Illinois has been underfunding its five state pension systems since at least the 1950s. During that period the legislature has also regularly been increasing benefits. For example, during the 1980s, statewide elected officials quietly sought amendments to the pension laws to change their base pay for pension benefits from that of the Speaker of the House to their own much higher salaries. Every biennium a thick pension bill has moved quietly through the legislative chambers, adding benefits for this or that group of employees. As a result, the combined unfunded liabilities of our pension and employee healthcare program reached over $120 billion, or 331 percent of the state's own source annual revenue (basically state revenue minus federal funding), which puts Illinois last among the fifty states on this measure.[17]

In December 2013 the General Assembly and governor enacted pension changes aimed at reducing pension liabilities and reducing the cost of state pensions to state government. The actions are tentative as of this writing, since state courts are weighing a challenge to the constitutionality of the changes. If upheld by the state's highest court, the changes will reduce annual state payments into the pension systems of $7.8 billion in FY2014 by about $1.2 billion. This would not, however, be enough to eliminate pressure on future budgets because the new pension financing plan still requires more spending as a portion of Illinois's revenues than is typical in other states. Nor would the savings of $1.2 billion eliminate projected future budget deficits. (See figure 5 on p. 26.)

Curbing Medicaid Spending

The formal federal-state split in funding of Medicaid is 50–50, yet the state captures additional federal dollars as a result of a complicated scheme in which the state taxes hospitals and the tax is then spent on Medicaid obligations, which generates additional federal matching funds. About three million residents are covered by Medicaid at a total cost of about $16 billion per year in 2014.

According to the Illinois Department of Healthcare and Family Services, 342,000 additional persons will be covered by Medicaid as a result of the federal Affordable Care Act (ACA).[18] In addition, about 140,000 persons who have been eligible for Medicaid but not enrolled can be expected to do so as a result of the publicity about the expanded program. Robert Kaestner and Nicole Kazee of the University of Illinois Institute of Government and Public Affairs project that the state's Medicaid obligations could grow between 10 percent and 20 percent by 2020 as a result of the ACA.[19]

Medicaid began with the Medicare program in 1965 and has been growing rapidly ever since. According to the Kaiser Family Foundation, Medicaid spending in Illinois grew by an average of 11.1 percent per year from 1990 to 2001; between 2001 and 2010 the annual rate of growth has been about 7 percent.[20] During these years state revenues were growing at about 3–4 percent per year, which contributes to the structural deficit described above in this chapter. See chapter 4 for a discussion of options for reducing Medicaid expenditures or at least slowing the rate in increase of spending for the program.

How Do We Get Out of This Mess?

The big question for Illinois policymakers in calendar year 2014 is whether to begin reducing the rates of the individual and corporate income taxes in 2015, as state statute requires, or to make the increases of 2011 permanent. The increased rates of the two taxes generate about $7.5 billion in annual revenue above that generated in 2010. Unfortunately, as noted above, the state had in the prior decade been spending and under-obligating for pensions about $7 billion a year, on average, more than the state had been taking in. Thus, the new revenues were almost completely absorbed in efforts to eliminate deficit spending.

The first steps in getting out of our fiscal mess are to reduce the rate of spending increase to less than the rate of inflation, and to increase the revenue from the present tax rates, or lower ones, at rates near or greater than that of inflation. Doing so would reverse the structural deficit under which the state's fiscal system has been suffering for decades. This requires, however, a restructuring of the State of Illinois revenue system, as discussed below.

Further, the present Illinois budget is inadequately analyzed, in part because lawmakers focus on a limited number of the state's funds. What if you had two bank accounts? One is in checking, for day-to-day and monthly expenses, with deposits from your paycheck. The other, in savings, is used for unexpected expenses and travel; the account receives substantial deposits from time to time from your old bachelor uncle who dotes on you.

Would a review solely of your checking account give an accurate picture of your financial position? Of course not, but that is basically how Illinois lawmakers review the state budget annually.[21] The lawmakers spend most of their budget review time examining the four General Funds, which account for about half of total state spending, while they basically ignore the seven hundred and ten funds that comprise the remainder of the $60 billion annual state budget.

The thinking is that the General Funds are the only sources of funds for discretionary spending. The hundreds of other state funds are seen as self-sustaining, which requires that the revenues streams be dedicated to the purpose for which the fund was created.

In reality, many of these other state funds receive up to 100 percent of their revenues as transfers from the General Funds. In other cases, some of their revenue streams are dedicated portions of general state taxes, most of which are part of the revenue streams of the General Funds. In addition, some of the General Funds revenues to support discretionary spending are transfers from other state funds. The Lottery and Gaming Funds transfer most of their "profits" to the General Funds to provide some of the discretionary spending support.

With transfers in and out of the General Funds to and from the other funds, sometimes with double counting, it is possible to obscure, distort, and manipulate budgetary actions. It is long been understood that the best way to protect the funding of a program is to get the spending transferred to an "other state fund" and create a statutory transfer, usually out of the General Funds to provide the necessary revenue to support it. For example, the state operating support for transit systems both for the Regional Transportation

Authority and the various Downstate systems occur in "other state funds," but all of the revenue to support these spending programs comes from transfers from the General Funds. Transfers made out of the General Funds represent spending, but the transfers are disguised from view and receive much less budgetary scrutiny. In its Fiscal Futures Model, the Institute of Government and Public Affairs at the University of Illinois has created a "Consolidated Funds Budget" that combines 80 of the largest of the state's funds for reporting purposes and provides a much more comprehensive picture of the state's fiscal situation.

2. Eliminate most of the transfers between state funds.

3. All revenues from state taxes (with the possible exception of transportation user fee taxes) should be deposited in the General Revenue Fund, and the spending should be appropriated from that fund.

4. Examine every fund to determine if there is any valid reason for its existence, focusing on the source of its revenue streams.

5. Consolidate a large number of state funds, at least for reporting purposes. This could significantly enhance the transparency of budgeting and eliminate the manipulations that can occur when only part of the budget is examined.

Management Improvements

In addition to fundamental changes in spending policies for pensions and Medicaid, which are discussed elsewhere in this and other chapters, there are management improvements that would assist the governor and lawmakers in crafting budgets. For example, we need to measure performance. If you don't measure what you do in state government, how do you know if you have done it well, and efficiently? Governor George Ryan (1999–2002) tried "performance measurement," but it was not implemented well, from what we are told by state employees. Agency divisions resisted creating performance measures for themselves and, if they did submit "measures," they were often indicators of activity rather than of the quality of the services provided. Lacking strong support from the governor's offices since the Ryan administration, use of performance measures has languished.

Mitch Daniels became governor of neighboring Indiana in 2005 and served until the end of 2012. Daniels is a believer in the adage "If you don't keep score, you're just practicing." Thus, one of his first actions was to create a Government Efficiency and Financial Planning (GEFP) unit in a new Office of Management and Budget. As unit director Christopher Johnston put it, "We became the 'management' in OMB."[22] Johnston and his five employees copied freely from the Program Assessment Rating Tool of the U.S. Office of Management and Budget to come up with eighteen questions that were asked of four hundred programs across more than seventy agencies. A key question asked in Indiana was, "Have specific long-term, results-based performance measures that are linked to the program purpose been established?" About half the programs had no measures whatever.

Agencies that resisted creating measures and achievement targets were told simply not to submit their budget requests to the State Budget Agency in OMB until they had done so. In other words, the governor was serious about performance management. Activity indicators such as the number of licenses an agency had processed were not accepted as performance measures. On the other hand, in the Department of Child Services the percentage of family reunifications achieved in less than twelve months was accepted as a key performance measure for one of the department's programs. Each program has from one to twenty performance measures. Up to three key performance indicators are reported to the governor's "dashboard," where he can quickly see agency performance. The dashboard is available to the public at results .in.gov.

Program management personnel determined what they thought to be satisfactory and superior levels of performance, and reports have been made quarterly to the GEFP unit for purposes of comparison and measurement of progress.

Performance measures are used at the front end in the biennial budgeting process and at the back end in the management of the agencies and programs. Indiana OMB director Adam Horst calls the program "performance-informed budgeting."[23] At the front end, the GEFP and the state budget agency, both part of OMB, eliminated funding for, among others, programs such as "value-added research" in the Department of Agriculture and "conservation and education outreach" in the Department of Conservation because they could neither generate performance measures or demonstrate any results. Use of the measures was also instrumental in dramatically increasing the efficiency of what had been an expensive children's home and in realigning programs such as lead paint removal, which had been conducted by two separate agencies until the programs were consolidated.

At the back end, the measures force agencies to think about what they do and how well they do it. The performance measures have become an invaluable management tool for Indiana state agencies and the state Office of Management and Budget.

According to Cristopher Johnston, a key to success is strong support from the governor, as many agencies are initially resistant to being measured. Further, Johnston says, the perfect should not be the enemy of the good. That is, start the performance program without waiting until a perfect plan has been developed, because that will never happen.

The Legislature has created a Budgeting for Results Commission, which has a long-term goal of performance measurement, but the commission seems to be moving slowly.

> 6. Create in the Illinois Governor's Office of Management and Budget a performance-informed budgeting program similar to that in Indiana.

Vendor Oversight

Most of the $22 billion expended by Illinois for health care and human services is distributed to nonprofit and for-profit health care providers and social service organizations, of which there are at least fifteen hundred that receive state funding. In June 2012 the *Chicago Tribune* reported that in the eighteen nonprofit social service organizations the newspaper studied, fourteen executives made more than the $150,000 paid to state cabinet-level officials who oversee the contracts given to the organizations.[24] Several were paid between $300,000 and $350,000 annually.

As steward of taxpayers' money, state government needs to better oversee the operations of the nongovernmental agencies that rely heavily, sometimes almost exclusively, on state dollars.

> 7. Create a uniform format for annual reporting to the Governor's Office of Management and Budget by all outside vendors that receive more than $1 million in annual revenue from the State of Illinois. As part of the annual report, agencies should be expected to provide performance measures and report on their performance on the measures.

Fees

During 2012, ninety state units administered 1,504 fees that generated $8.2 billion in revenues and represent the fourth-largest source of revenue in the state budget, following the federal government, individual income tax, and sales tax.[25] Fees range from those on persons licensed to do business or practice their professions in Illinois to public university tuitions to those imposed by the Secretary of State, amounting to 495 fees, including drivers' licenses and motor vehicle registration fees, across twenty administrative units.

Illinois exceeded national averages in fees related to vehicle usage, while collecting less than the national average in other fees. Vehicle-related fees include motor vehicle and vehicle operators' licenses, tolls, and other highway fees. Per capita vehicle fees in Illinois of $185.47 were $85 greater than the national average.[26] This in part reflects the fact that Illinois is one of thirteen states that collect significant toll revenues (more than $100 million in Illinois). The state's per capita vehicle fees ranked highest among a comparison of thirteen large or neighboring states. Fees from sources other than those related to motor vehicles were lower overall than in the average state.

Many fees were raised dramatically in 2003, during the first year of Rod Blagojevich's tenure, often by more than 100 percent. Most fees now bear little or no relation to the cost of providing the service for which a fee is imposed and have become business taxes on selected segments of the state population.

8. Begin a program, administered by the Auditor General, to conduct activity cost–based analyses of the cost of providing fee-based services to Illinois businesses and residents. Fees could then be adjusted to cover only the cost of providing state services in each fee category. The program could begin with the occupations and professions, for which fees were doubled and trebled in 2003.

An Appropriate Revenue System for Illinois

What should be the principles for taxation? We adhere to those provided by the Tax Foundation, in Washington, D.C., a business group.[27] A tax should be relatively simple to administer, and it should be transparent, that is, fully explained and understandable by the public. A tax should be neutral and not favor or discriminate against any business or activity; some economists prefer what they call "equity" instead, which calls for basing tax rates on the ability to pay, with higher rates on higher incomes. At the state level, we prefer flat-rate taxation instead, with individual exemptions for low-income earners. Finally, taxes should be broad-based and set at a low rate. In this regard, lawmakers should avoid enacting targeted deductions, credits and exclusions, other than to avoid the pyramiding of a tax burden or to avoid double taxation.

Since about 1970, Illinois has had a tendency to rely on tax rate changes to provide revenue increases in times of need. In times of economic growth or inflation, when revenues have been in excess of need, exemptions or exclusions from the tax base have been incorporated into our tax system. These actions are called "tax expenditures," that is, exemptions or exclusions that reduce the amount of tax revenue that would otherwise accrue to the state. In 2011, according to the Illinois Office of the Comptroller, tax expenditures cost Illinois government $6.78 billion.[28]

In addition, the income and sales taxes are imposed on rather narrow bases. This has resulted in a tax system that is less responsive to economic growth than is ideal. For example, the sales tax base is now 25 percent dependent solely on the sales of motor fuel and vehicles. And the exemption for food for home consumption has made the tax more unstable in times of economic contraction. The exemption of retirement income from the income tax base has eliminated the fastest-growing portion of personal income. Illinois is one of only three states that exempt all qualified retirement plan income from taxation. (Nine states do not impose a tax on income.)

Illinois also provides a 5 percent tax credit against our state income tax for property taxes paid. Because many of us use income tax preparers, we never see the credit, and few people think of the credit on income taxes as relief of their property tax bills. The revenue lost is about half a billion dollars.

Illinois has a rather typical revenue system, but one slightly more dependent on revenue sources that reflect little of natural economic growth or price and income growth. For example, cigarette and liquor tax revenues generally only respond to consumption and not price growth. Illinois's tax on fuel, natural gas, and electricity are all based on consumption levels as well.

The state sales tax is imposed on most goods such as automobiles and refrigerators but is not imposed on automotive repair or appliance repair services. Illinois exempts most services from the sales tax, though the service sector has grown to be much larger than the goods sector.

The Illinois corporate income tax rate is now the fourth-highest in the nation, though only about one-third of corporations pay the tax. Most corporations are small and owner-managed, generating under $1 million in annual revenues. The owners often pay themselves bonuses from the profits, if any, so no corporate income tax liability remains. In addition, many corporations are now legally organized to pass income through to partners and shareholders. Nevertheless, the high rate sticks out like a sore thumb.

See chapter 5 for further discussion of this issue and for the recommendation that Illinois immediately reduce the rate of its corporate income tax from 9.5 percent to no more than 7.3 percent, the rate prior to the 2011 income tax increases.

Base-Broadening Revenue Options for Consideration

Here we discuss briefly two examples of base broadening: extending the sales tax to services and reimposition of the sales tax on food for home consumption.

The Illinois sales tax is imposed by the state at the rate of 6.25 percent. The state retains 5 percent, and 1.25 percent is distributed to municipalities and counties. Home rule cities and counties may impose additional local sales taxes, and in some locales in Cook County the total sales tax rate is almost 10 percent. The aggregate state and local sales tax rate in Illinois, an amalgam of different local rates, is 7.5 percent, significantly higher than the national median state and local sales tax rate of 6.8 percent.[29] But the tax is imposed, as noted above, on a narrow base of goods and not generally on services. Illinois taxes 17 services, mostly in the utilities category, in contrast to 160 services that are taxed in Hawaii and 94 in neighboring Iowa.[30] Washington State and New Mexico each tax 158 services. These include personal services such as hairstyling, admissions to amusements such as movies, and repair services.

In 1950 goods represented 60 percent of all personal consumption expenditures, with services representing the other 40 percent. By 2010, however, the relationship was reversed and services represented 67 percent of personal consumption and goods just 33 percent.[31] As a result, the narrow Illinois sales tax base grows more slowly than the economy as a whole. Adjusted for inflation, sales tax revenues have remained virtually flat since 1985.[32] Excluding most services from the sales tax is regressive; that is, low-income persons spend a higher percentage of their income on goods than do high-income persons, while the latter spend more of their income on services. By extending the sales tax to certain personal, amusement, and consumer services, the state could generate enough revenue to reduce the present 6.25 percent rate and also create a fairer tax overall.

A sales tax on some services would create an overall sales tax that would grow at about the same rate as the economy, something the narrow tax on goods does not do. This change would reduce pressure on the annual state budget and reduce the need for periodic increases in the rates of major state taxes. The Illinois Commission on Government Forecasting and Accountability has estimated that if all services in Illinois were taxed, excluding business-to-business sales, Illinois would generate about $4 billion in additional revenue.[33]

The state sales tax has over the years also become riddled with exemptions. The biggest is for food for home consumption and drugs. If we eliminated the exemption on food for home consumption, Illinois would generate $1.5

billion dollars in annual revenue. The exemption for food was thought to be fairer to poor people, who expend a greater percentage of their income for food than do those better off. However, most poor people take advantage of the Supplemental Nutrition Assistance Program (SNAP, which used to be known as food stamps), which is not taxed anyway, so there is no benefit to the poor on SNAP purchases. Yet at about the time the exemption for home consumption was instituted in the 1980s, the overall sales tax rate had to be increased by 1 percentage point to make up for revenue lost by exempting food for home consumption from the sales tax, and of course the poor do pay the higher sales tax on other goods.

Ryan Aprill has shown that more than 80 percent of the tax exemption benefit accrues to the top 60 percent of income earners.[34] Aprill suggests that it would make better tax policy to tax food for home consumption, reduce the overall sales tax rate, and provide a rebate or credit to low-income households against their taxes paid.

In table 3 we have provided illustrations of possible base-broadening revenue options that are available to policymakers. Keep in mind that base-broadening can result in tax rate reductions and may make the tax structure more stable and growth oriented.

There is an old adage in politics: Once something is given, it is never taken back. Eliminating tax expenditures and imposing sales tax on services would thus probably be as difficult as making the 2011 income tax rate increases permanent, if not more so. Yet these structural reforms would create a revenue system that might allow for reductions in the existing rates of our major taxes.

TABLE 3. Base-broadening revenue increase options ($ in millions)

Reimpose sales tax on food for home consumption	$1,500
Tax retirement income, excluding Social Security income	$1,780
Eliminate property tax credit on income tax	$540
Impose sales tax on nonprofit organizations	$420
Exempt vehicle trade-ins	$310
Tax all other tax expenditures*	$3,240
Tax sales on wide array of services	$4,000
Total revenue impact of eliminating tax expenditures and taxing services	$11,790

Note: *A tax expenditure is any exemption, exclusion, deduction, allowance, credit, preferential tax rate, abatement, or other device that reduces the amount of tax revenue that would otherwise accrue to the state.

Source: Illinois Department of Revenue; Office of the Comptroller; Governor's Office of Management and Budget. Calculations are by the authors.

For years, Illinois has spent and obligated far more than it has been generating in revenue. In order for the state to balance its budgets honestly in the future, it will have to curb the rate of growth in Medicaid and social services spending and, ideally, reform the revenue system to make it more responsive to economic growth.

CHAPTER 3

Upgrading Education

Education is arguably the most important function of state and local governments. The schools and universities provide the foundation on which the success or failure of society rests. This chapter begins with an overview of the scope, organization, and recent performance of K–12 education in Illinois. We then discuss Illinois's convoluted system of state funding of local schools and go on to examine options for change in education within a context of constrained resources. The chapter ends with the topic of higher education and the whirlwind of change being caused largely by online education.

Illinois enrolls 3 million students in education, from pre-kindergarten through graduate research training at public universities. This accounts for almost one in four of the 12.9 million residents of the state.[1] More than 2.3 million youngsters enrolled in public and private pre-kindergarten through twelfth grade in 2012, and in the same year 847,000 students signed up for higher education. Illinois governments spent $30 billion on education in 2011, more than 4 percent of the state's gross domestic product.

After decades in which Illinois ranked in the middle or lower range among the states in financial support for kindergarten through high school (K–12) public education, the state and local school districts showed strong support for public education from the 1990s to 2012. In 1992, for example, Illinois state and local governments spent $4,866 per pupil compared with a national average of $5,097 and ranked twenty-third among the fifty states. By 2012, however, Illinois spending per pupil had jumped to $12,368, improving its ranking to seventeenth, and was higher than the national average of $10,976.[2] The figure is misleading, however, because spending for Illinois schools is spread unevenly across property-rich and property-poor districts; as a result, two-thirds of Illinois school districts actually spend less than the national average.[3]

Public school enrollment has declined from a high of 2.37 million pupils in 1972 to 2.1 million in 2012.[4] Minorities represented 28.8 percent of enrollees in 1981, yet a generation later, in 2012, they represented half of the total, with blacks and Latinos each representing more than 20 percent of total enrollment. Nearly three in ten public school students came from low-income families in 1991; by 2012, 49 percent of public school students were classified as low-income.

Many families eschew the public system. Private schools play a large though declining role in the education of children. Private schools enrolled 14 percent of all elementary and secondary students in 1994 but only 10 percent in 2012. Private school enrollments have declined sharply from 320,290 in 1994 to 233,800 in 2012.[5] Still, in 2010 there were 1,141 private schools throughout Illinois, and in 2012 the Catholic Archdiocese of Chicago alone enrolled 86,500 students in 255 schools.[6]

The number of families educating their children at home has grown sharply in recent years, although no one seems to know the extent of this increase. Illinois requires only that home school families register their children with their regional office of education, though there is no assurance that all do so. As a result, the Illinois State Board of Education (ISBE) is unwilling to hazard a guess as to how many children in Illinois are schooled at home. At the national level, about 1.5 million students were home-schooled in 2007, according to the National Center for Education Statistics.[7] If Illinois is close to the average, the state would have about 75,000 students who are schooled at home.[8]

Illinois public schools exist in a tangle of state, intermediate, and local administrative units. The governor appoints the nine-member State Board of Education from the state's five appellate court districts; the ISBE in turn appoints a state superintendent of education who oversees a staff of five hundred with offices in Springfield, Chicago, and Mt. Vernon. In addition, 41 independent, elected Illinois Regional Office of Education superintendents throughout the state support the ISBE and operate their own independent programs in support of local school districts. At the local level, 867 school districts elect seven-member boards, which operate K–12, elementary, or high school districts.

In 1942 there were twelve thousand elementary school districts in Illinois, most with a single one-room schoolhouse per district.[9] Some counties had more school board members than teachers. Increased state aid and persistent efforts by groups including the Illinois Farm Bureau cut the number of districts in half by 1948. Consolidation continued in the 1950s, with the total falling to two thousand districts, and further decline reduced the number to 867 in 2012, which is still far more districts than most states have.

School districts are organized into three types: unit districts, which cover grades K–12 (there are 390 of them); elementary districts, which are responsible only for K–8 students (377), and high school districts (99); the latter two types are called "dual districts" because the high school districts each overlie one or more elementary districts. In LaSalle County, for example, seven separate elementary districts feed into one high school district.

Because of tradition and emotional ties, many if not most board members of dual districts resist consolidation into unit districts. Nevertheless, mergers of the 377 elementary districts into 99 high school districts should save significantly on administrative overhead and generate other efficiencies. In addition, the elementary school curricula and pedagogy could be coordinated more effectively with the high school or high schools in a unit district.

> 9. Consolidate Illinois's 377 elementary districts into their 99 overlying high school districts.

Mired in the Middle

School organization is probably less important to achievement than are the quality of teaching, richness of the school program, length of school day and year, and other factors.

Achievement in Illinois public schools is strongly correlated with income. The research and advocacy group Advance Illinois reports that in 2011 only 16 percent of low-income fourth-grade students read proficiently, while 49 percent of those who were not low-income read proficiently.[10] The same wide gap existed that year for proficiency in eighth-grade math between students who were low-income and students who were not.

So is it reasonable to report on statewide averages in achievement in Illinois when there is such diversity in income and test scores? Is there any value in averaging scores from high-achieving New Trier schools in prosperous Winnetka, with almost no low-income people, and the Chicago public schools, where 80 percent of the students now qualify as low-income?

The answer is probably no, yet about the only way national statistics are gathered is on a statewide basis, and so that is how observers compare them. Further, states have a responsibility to educate all students, so achievement throughout the whole state may be a measure, albeit a very rough one, of how well Illinois and other states are doing their jobs.

Illinois is also an average kind of state. In 2007, for example, the Associated Press named Illinois "the most average state" in the nation, based on twenty-one demographic and economic factors. According to the AP, "Illinois' racial composition matches the nation's better than of any other state. Education levels are similar, as are the mix of industry and the percentage of immigrants."[11]

Thus Illinois can be expected to score about average on nationwide tests of academic achievement. And for the most part it does. In 2011, 34 percent of Illinois eighth graders received a score of proficient or above in reading, and 33 percent did so in math.[12] This placed Illinois far below top-scoring Massachusetts, where 46 percent were proficient or above in reading and 51 percent in math. Illinois ranked right in the middle among the fifty states. In its 2013 statistical analysis of a number of educational achievement indicators, *Education Week* magazine gave Illinois a C+ overall, which was the national average grade.[13]

Nonetheless, 59 percent of respondents to a 2011 Illinois survey rated their local schools as good or excellent, and only 19 percent rated their schools poor or very poor, with 22 percent rating the schools fair.[14] This generally favorable view by the public of its schools will make it challenging for leaders in the area of education to increase expectations for higher achievement in the future.

On measures of college readiness Illinois fares poorly, along with many other states. According to Advance Illinois, this is reflected in low postsecondary enrollment rates (just 40 percent of high school freshmen enroll in postsecondary schools), high remediation rates (nearly half of community college students require at least one remedial course), and insufficient postsecondary attainment rates (38 percent of Illinois adults hold an associate's degree or higher at a time when eight of every ten jobs require such training).[15] Compounding the challenge is the increasing cost of postsecondary education. According to Advance Illinois, it costs an average family 21 percent of its income to send a student to a four-year public university, making Illinois one of the least affordable states for college in the country.[16]

We turn next to school funding in Illinois, which needs a lot of improvement.

State School Aid Formula: Convoluted and Opaque

In the 2011–12 school year, total state, local, and federal funding for Illinois public schools amounted to $28.7 billion. Of that amount, $15.8 billion, or

55 percent, came from the local property tax; $9.3 billion, or 32.4 percent, was from the state, and $3.5 billion (12.5 percent) came from the federal government.[17] This places Illinois among the bottom ten states in terms of state support for education as a percentage of total funding; the national average is 45 percent from state sources.[18] Until the 1920s, local property taxes provided almost the sole source of funding for Illinois public schools. This led to severe inequities, as districts varied greatly in their property wealth per pupil. In 1927 the state created a program of "equalization" in which the state provided financial support on a formula basis to property-poor districts.[19] The formula set a "foundation level" of funding per pupil that every district would receive from a combination of local and state revenues.

If local property taxes alone provided more than the foundation level for a district, it would receive only a nominal amount. For districts whose local taxes failed to reach the foundation level of per-pupil support, the state would provide the difference in order to bring every district up to the foundation level. That has been the basic concept in state funding for local schools—until recently.

As noted above, the state share of public school funding is much less than in most states, yet it still amounts to about 50 percent of all funding for districts other than the high-property-wealth districts that can fund their programs solely with local property taxes. Nevertheless, Illinois has one of the greatest disparities among the states in per-pupil funding between low-property-wealth districts and those with high property wealth. During the 2009–10 academic year, the wealthiest elementary districts in Illinois spent about $24,000 per pupil while the poorest districts spent about $6,000.[20] These districts are outliers, but a 2010 study found that Illinois has the second-highest disparity in the nation between property-poor and property-wealthy districts.[21] A 2012 report from the Education Law Center at Rutgers University accorded Illinois one of three F grades among the states for funding distribution.[22] The report noted that in 2009 local schools with zero poverty-level students expended $2,600 more per pupil than did schools with 30 percent poverty-level enrollees.

In 1997 the state board of education created the Education Funding Advisory Board (EFAB), made up of school experts. The purpose of EFAB was to establish an objective level of per-pupil funding that would be adequate to provide a minimally acceptable education. In 2002 it set a foundation level of $4,560, which the state funded.[23] Since that year, however, Illinois has failed to fund the annual board-established foundation levels. In 2012, EFAB set the minimally acceptable funding level at $8,360 per pupil, but state funding supported a foundation of only $6,119 per pupil. For fiscal year 2013, the state reduced general state aid by $519 million, or 11 percent of the preceding year's total, about $259 per pupil statewide. For 2014, the 11 percent reduction is expected to remain in place.

Instead of reducing state aid to schools on a per-pupil basis or on some progressive basis that cut funding for poor schools less than it cut support for better-funded ones, the state board of education decided to cut each school district by the same 11 percent. In 2012 Illinois allocated, on average about $3,391 for each of its two million public school students. But few receive the average. For example, in 2010–11 Kankakee School District 111 received $4,875 per pupil in general state aid, while New Trier High on Chicago's suburban North Shore received only $218 per pupil in general state aid (New Trier received an additional $518 per pupil from categorical grants such as those for transportation and special education). Even with all the state aid it received, Kankakee expended only about $11,663 per pupil while New Trier, with its high property wealth, spent $20,807 per pupil, largely derived from property taxes. Yet because 2012 funding was reduced by the same 11 percent from each district's previous year's level of General State Aid, Kankakee saw a reduction of about $536 per pupil and New Trier had a cut of only about $24 per pupil.

10. When it is necessary to reduce state school aid to school districts, do so on a statewide per-pupil basis or on some progressive basis that reduces funding for poorly funded schools less than for wealthier districts.

There is an old saying that only six people really understand the Illinois state school aid formula, and they are not allowed to travel on the same plane. The formula has become even more complex in recent decades with the introduction of two elements into the General State Aid formula that are unrelated to "equalization." These are the poverty grant and the Property Tax Extension Limitation Law (PTELL) subsidy.[24]

The poverty grant assumes that schools with a high percentage of low-income students face more expensive challenges in educating these students, many of whom are at risk of failure. In 1999 the formula for identifying low-income students changed and the formula for determining the size of the grant per student changed as well, which resulted in a dramatic increase in funding for schools with high percentages of low-income students. In just twelve years, the poverty grant more than quadrupled, from $295 million in 2000 to $1.57 billion in 2012.[25]

The PTELL subsidy provides property tax relief to school districts where property tax extensions (local revenues) are capped by the limitation law.

Many of these districts have seen their property tax wealth grow over the years, yet they are not able to capture the growth in increased local property tax revenue, absent voter referenda. The subsidy replaces what the districts with growth would have generated locally had they not been limited by the PTELL. This subsidy grew from just $46 million in 2000 to $780 million in 2009 and then fell with declining home values to $629 million in 2012, still an increase of 1,267 percent.

Why do the poverty grant and PTELL subsidy matter? Because they take monies away from what would earlier have gone into the foundation level grants of the general state aid formula, which are based solely on property wealth "equalization." There has actually been a decline in state funding for the foundation grants, from $2.61 billion in 2000 to $2.45 billion in 2012.

Both the poverty grant and the PTELL subsidy are buried in the general state aid (GSA) line of the Illinois State Budget, and thus are understood by just a handful of Illinois lawmakers and policy analysts. We are not against poverty grants and property tax relief as such. We wonder, however, if state legislators had known about the dramatic growth in these two programs, would they have approved such growth at the expense of the original purpose of the GSA equalization grant? For example, if the PTELL subsidy were eliminated as of 2009 and the money devoted to the equalization grants, the foundation level would have increased from $5,959 to $6,678, much closer to the assumed EFAB-recommended amount that year of $7,128.

The primary beneficiary of these changes in the school aid formula is the Chicago public school district, which admittedly faces daunting challenges. Sixty-four percent of the PTELL subsidy ($505 million) and 52 percent of the poverty grant ($582 million) went to Chicago schools in 2009. As a result of these programs, Chicago has seen its education property tax rate drop from $3.60 per $100 of equalized assessed valuation (EAV) in 2001 to $2.37 in 2009 (the latest year available). The $2.37 tax rate for Chicago compares with rates of $3 to $6 per $100 of EAV in school districts elsewhere in Illinois.

Special education is another line item in the state budget that deserves review and possible adjustment. Chicago receives a single block grant based on the ratio of special education costs in Chicago to those in the rest of Illinois in 1995. In 2009, that split generated approximately $9,100 per special education pupil in Chicago and only about $3,324 for every such pupil in the rest of Illinois's school districts.

Again, we emphasize that Chicago may deserve all it receives from the state, yet we have an uneasy feeling that the Chicago public schools may not be making enough local tax effort in behalf of its schools relative to the effort of most other districts.

11. Separate the PTELL property tax relief subsidy and the poverty grant from the annual General State Aid allocation to provide transparency.

12. Phase out the PTELL property tax subsidy and review the dramatic growth in the poverty grant.

13. Reevaluate the special education funding formula in Illinois to assure that funds are being allocated statewide on an equitable basis.

The present school funding system is at best deeply opaque, and it has been worsened by special funding programs that are unrelated to local district property tax wealth, the original purpose of the GSA formula. The funding system also has the effect of bringing down local tax rates (and thus "effort") in many school districts that have experienced significant growth in their local property wealth and are under property tax caps. In effect, the districts where property wealth is growing benefit from higher general state aid while districts that have not shown any growth in property values shoulder significantly higher property tax rates, which seems unfair to us.

14. Rewrite the General State Aid school funding formula to align it more closely with the original objective of reducing the disparities in per-pupil funding between property-poor and property-wealthy districts.

Suggestions for Educational Policy Change

As was detailed in chapter 2, on budgeting, Illinois spending for education will be constrained in the coming years by a state budget that is burdened with debt and unfunded obligations. Several of the following recommendations will require additional resources, which will not be forthcoming until the state budget is stabilized.

When the authors were schoolboys in the 1940s and '50s, we went to school from 8:15 to 3:20 each day. A check with several Illinois school superintendents finds that the schedule is similar today. Excluding lunch and time spent passing from class to class, that amounts to 6 hours of instructional time per day. School is in session in Illinois about 176 days per year. The state requires a minimum of 880 hours of schooling each year, or five hours per day; Texas requires 1,260 hours, or 7 hours per day. Chicago public schools have had one of the shortest school days in the country, at 5 hours and 9 minutes; it was extended to 7 hours in 2012–13 through the leadership of Chicago mayor Rahm Emanuel.

Many public charter schools in Illinois have longer school days than the 6 hours typical of the regular public schools, with up to 90 minutes of reading and math each day instead of the 45 minutes devoted to those critical subjects in most public schools. Japanese children go to school 7 hours per day for 240 days per year, and German children attend school for 210 days each year.[26]

We don't know the optimal number of hours and days of class time for our schoolchildren, but we surmise that more time on lessons taught by stimulating teachers will generate more learning. There must be a point, however, at which the limited attention spans of youngsters will reach sharply diminishing returns. Maybe the Japanese children go to school too much.

Then there is the issue of the traditional three-month summer vacation. Many teachers report that they spend several weeks at the beginning of each school year reviewing what was learned the preceding year—and forgotten over the summer.[27]

> 15. Move to a year-round school calendar, with a one-month break in the winter and a one-month vacation in the summer, for about 200 days each year, and have school days 6½ to 7 hours long.

Salary Differentials

At present, there are no salary differentials among teachers on the basis of the subject matter they teach. This makes it hard to attract good math and science teachers. There is a surplus of physical education teachers and those in disciplines less rigorous than math and science. Natural rules of supply and demand tell us that math and science teachers should be paid more than those in disciplines with a more than adequate supply of teachers.

> 16. Negotiate salary differentials by subject matter area in public school bargaining contracts.

Master Teachers

There are about 150,000 teachers in Illinois public schools. Most would benefit from interacting with "master teachers." Illinois teachers can earn this status by completing the National Board Certification program, which is a rigorous challenge that requires a major investment of a teacher's time and personal resources.

According to *State Legislatures* magazine: "Because these teachers have met high standards through study, expert evaluation, self-assessment and peer review, schools and districts believe master teachers will improve student learning, contribute to a new, positive school culture, and become powerful teacher leaders."[28] The number of master teachers in Chicago rose from 11 in 2000 to 1,100 by 2008. As of 2008, nine in ten board-certified teachers had stayed in the Chicago public schools, and 50 percent held leadership positions within their schools.[29]

Illinois provided $11.5 million in fiscal year 2009 to support teachers who were working toward their certification. That amount has dropped to just $1 million in the 2014 budget. We feel that the program is so important to teachers and schools that funding should be restored to the 2009 level.

17. Restore master teacher support funding to the previous level of $11.5 million.

Principal Mentoring

Research is showing that the school principal (the term comes from "principal teacher") can lead the process of improving instruction in his or her building.[30] According to a 2010 report by the Chicago Community Trust, "[o]ver the past decade it has become increasingly clear that even the lowest performing school can be dramatically improved if a committed and competent principal assumes instructional leadership and is supported by the district in doing so."[31]

And here the numbers are manageable. There are about 3,800 principals and 2,500 assistant principals in Illinois public schools. About 10 percent of these administrators turn over every year. From 2007 to 2011 the General Assembly required that new principals receive mentoring, generally from active or recently retired principals, and provided funding therefor. The legislature eliminated funding for the program in 2012. At present there is no state-supported professional development for principals. Given the central importance of the principal in the education process, we believe that this lack of support for principals is an unfortunate oversight and should be rectified, even in a context of tight budgets.

18. Restore funding for the statewide principal mentoring program.

Charter Schools

Charter public schools are all the rage among education reformers and business leaders. In Illinois such schools are authorized by local public school districts under a charter (typically five years) to provide education that often is somewhat specialized in science, mathematics, or the arts, for example. In 2011 the Illinois State Board of Education was also authorized by the legislature to grant charters on appeals from local charter organizers who had been denied charters by the local school district.

We visited the Quest Charter School Academy Peoria in February 2011. The academy focuses on math, science, and technology. The techniques employed there are not magic—a longer school day and school year, twice as much time devoted to math and English as in regular schools, strong parental involvement, and high expectations.

The Quest Academy operates in a previously shuttered public elementary school. About 700 students applied in 2010 for the 225 slots in a school for grades five to seven that is extending its ambit each year until it provides education through the senior year of high school. Students, who were selected by lottery, reflect the demographics of the Peoria school district.

As a charter, Quest can operate independent of most school district rules. Teachers are, for example, on yearly contracts rather than protected from firing by tenure. Nevertheless, Quest received four hundred résumés for its twenty teaching positions. As its principal, Engin Blackstone, noted, "We can change things overnight if they aren't working to our satisfaction."

Quest receives about the same amount of funding per pupil as do the regular public schools in Peoria. The school is operated by Concept Schools, a nonprofit that runs 25 schools in Midwestern states, primarily in Ohio.

As we see it, the key differences between Quest and Peoria's regular schools are these:

- Each Quest school day is 62 minutes longer, and after-school activities in chess club, MathCounts, the science fair, and other competitive pursuits are encouraged; after-school tutoring is also available.
- Math and English are taught for 90 minutes per day each, rather than 45 minutes.
- School is held on Saturdays for students who are struggling and for advanced students.
- The school year is eight days longer, and school is held with volunteers from area colleges when teachers are occupied by required professional development (normally, students are let off during what we used to call "Institute" days).
- Parental involvement is emphasized; there are four rather than the typical two parent conferences, held on Saturdays, and home visits by teach-advisors are required.[32]

The first years of state test results for Quest are encouraging. The school performed significantly better in 2011 and 2012 than did the Peoria School District and a little better than the state average.

The big question is whether charter schools make a difference in outcomes, now that there are five thousand of them nationwide educating 1.5 million students (there are 115 in Illinois, with 42,000 students, or about 2 percent of the state's public school students).[33] A recent major evaluation by the U.S. Department of Education found that, "[o]n average, charter middle schools that hold lotteries are neither more nor less successful than traditional schools in improving student achievement, behavior and school progress."[34] A meta-analysis of research studies of charters found in 2011 that charters were better at teaching elementary school reading and mathematics and middle-school math; a study in Massachusetts concluded that urban charter schools are effective for minorities, poor students, and low achievers.[35]

The most successful charter schools are operated by the KIPP network (formerly the Knowledge Is Power Program), which operates 125 schools in twenty states. In many ways, KIPP schools operate as the Quest Academy does, with longer school days and years than regular public schools have. A rigorous five-year study of forty-three KIPP schools by Mathematica Policy Research found that "[t]he average impact of KIPP on student achievement is positive, statistically significant, and educationally substantial."[36] Ninety-five percent of KIPP's open-enrollment, inner-city middle-school students graduate from high school, and 33 percent graduate from four-year colleges and universities, many more than similar students in regular public schools.[37]

Many other charter schools fail, however, to live up to the dreams of their founders and should be shuttered.

Today, in more and more states, students and parents are also offered a smorgasbord of choices outside the local public school system: vouchers to attend private schools, the right to choose another public school inside or outside the local district, and the option of attending courses at the area community college.

Governor Mitch Daniels of neighboring Indiana went to the head of the class in 2012, if you will, in terms of ambitious changes according to which state money follows the student to any of several options, in addition to charter schools, that may seem best for the student and his or her parents. The Daniels plan will soon make vouchers of money available to any student of low- and low-to-middle income status to go to private nonprofit, religious, and for-profit schools. For high school students, there is no limit on the tuition that the government will spend so long as the student meets the means-testing. And if Indiana students apply to public schools outside their neighborhood and district, their school funding will follow them. This open enrollment option has been in place in Iowa since 1989 and has worked well in that state, according to Jeff Burger, deputy state education superintendent in Iowa.[38]

Other options have been developing in Illinois. Juniors and seniors in Nowlan's rural school district in Stark County, southeast of the Quad Cities, are taking college-credit courses at the high school through a branch of Black Hawk College, a two-year institution. Students earn both high school and college credits, and for some students it amounts to earning up to a year's worth of college credits while in high school. This makes it possible for some students to graduate from college in three years. Thirty-eight percent of all juniors and seniors at the high school are enrolled in college-credit courses. These "dual credit" programs are found throughout Illinois and have been a plus for small rural districts that lack the resources to offer the Advanced Placement courses (also for college credit) that are popular in suburban schools.

Online instruction is also transforming American education. This could improve efficiency, reduce costs, and most important, help students. Without accountability and oversight, however, the promise might exceed the performance. Here is how it works in Illinois. Tucked away in a storefront in a tiny village outside Peoria is a school, the Illinois Virtual School, that teaches British Literature, Advanced Placement calculus, Mandarin, and Arabic, among more than one hundred courses for middle and high school students. The courses come to students throughout the state, rather than the other way around, via the Internet, of course.

Two hundred of the state's 867 school districts "send" students to the virtual school, and three thousand course enrollments were recorded in 2012–13. Districts that are participating range from tiny rural districts to the Chicago public schools. Many large districts operate their own online education programs.

Courses are offered fourteen times per year, so the student who finds in March that she lacks one course for graduation from high school can sign up; if she pushes herself, she can finish the course in time to graduate. And, of course, there are the rural schools that cannot find or afford the advanced science, foreign language, or math teachers and thus can sign their students up for the rich offerings from the state virtual school.

Tuition is $250 per course, which we figure is roughly one-third what it costs a school district to offer a course in its school; the virtual school budget is, however, supplemented by the Illinois State Board of Education. About half the schools pay the tuition; the other half require the student to pay.

Students register online at ilvirtual.org. A "learning management system" at the virtual school provides the course materials, assignments, and connections to the teacher for the course. If books and science kits are needed, the Illinois Virtual School (IVS) sends them out.

At the IVS there is constant feedback from the teacher, who is almost always available, if not immediately, then soon after being requested. Students put their completed work in an electronic "drop box," which the teacher accesses to pick up the work and grade it. Each teacher has a homepage for communication with the students. There is also a discussion board at which students can communicate with other students and their teacher. Students work at their own pace, yet must finish within the seventeen-week semester. Eighty-three percent of the students at IVS in 2012–13 completed their courses with a passing grade.

Illinois is actually a small-time player in online education at the moment. A majority of the other states have full-time online schools, whereas the IVS simply supplements what schools offer. Arizona has thirty-seven thousand students in full-time online settings, Ohio thirty-one thousand, and Pennsylvania twenty-nine thousand.

19. Expand school choice options in Illinois. Evaluate the experiences of neighboring Indiana, Iowa, and elsewhere to include public charter schools, vouchers to attend private schools, and open enrollment in districts other than the one in which a student resides. The choice programs that fail to show adequate academic achievement should be closed. The others should be allowed to flourish.

The biggest challenge facing American education, and certainly that in Illinois, is finding ways to increase expectations significantly among parents, communities, and students. Simply doing as well as the school and students down the highway or in the neighboring suburb is no longer good enough. The next governor of Illinois will have to devote himself or herself to conveying to all the seriousness of the challenges we face in competing with the many nations that have surpassed us in academic achievement. Either that, or our nation will have to import much of its well-educated workforce, for whom most of the rest of us will be working in years to come.

We now turn to our colleges and universities, where we have a good mix of public, private, nonprofit, and for-profit institutions that are struggling to cope in an era of constrained resources.

Lessons from Friday Night Football

My rural high school is in the 2013 fall football playoffs, and the frenzy in town is palpable.

Can we learn anything from the intense focus on high school sports that could benefit the academic side of high school? I have some ideas.

Recently, I drove the several miles to the neighboring town to the playoff game. My rural town is consolidated with another town into one school district, as is common in depopulating rural Illinois.

The consolidation, long staunchly opposed by most, came about in large part because one fall one of the schools lacked enough players to field a competitive football team!

Along the highway to the playing field elaborate signs, painted by parents and students, exhorted the team to greater glory for the local area.

At the high school, the student lockers of football players are emblazoned with signs that proclaim their team membership, making them part of the in crowd. Football standouts are lionized by students and community alike. One-third of all the high school boys are on the football team.

In contrast, school sports are not part of education in most countries I know of, so parents overseas can focus attention on their children's academic progress.

Yet school sports are valuable, in moderation, and I think other countries are missing something. Think of the stimulating competition and the team-building values of girls' volleyball and basketball, something not available to girls when I went to school, lo those many decades ago.

My high school's football team is very good, and strong teams have become a tradition. But the academics in the school are mediocre at best.

American College Testing (ACT) scores are barely at the state average. The results would be way below average if the scores of Chicago's struggling public high schoolers were eliminated from the state averages. ACT scores locally haven't moved in a decade.

So can we channel some of the community and parental energy now devoted to sports into academics? I think so.

In the 1920s and '30s, my high school participated in a day-long county track and field—*and* declamation—meet.

After the track and field events were over, the declamation contest was held, at which a girl and a boy from each school gave a speech. The speech scores were an integral part of the track and field scoring, and they often determined which school won the overall meet.

The speeches were a big deal, according to a local historian; big crowds attended. The school yearbooks devoted as much space to the speeches as to the exploits of the runners on the track.

I think a key to the intense interest in high school sports—and declamation in the past—lies in competition with area schools.

So here is my idea.

We should initiate competition among high schools based on academics. We already have in place conferences of schools of similar size and socioeconomic status.

And since 1900 we have had the Illinois High School Association, which sanctions and oversees sports as well as competitions in music, speech, debate, and even bass fishing. The IHSA is overseen by high school principals, so we have the infrastructure to direct the academic competition.

Schools would compete on the basis of their scores on the ACT (which every Illinois high schooler takes), so every student would feel involved.

In addition, the speech, science Olympiad, and scholastic bowl teams would compete within the conference. Scores from those events would be added to the outcomes of the ACT scores.

Possibly the speech and other academic clubs could hold a single major conference meet in order to heighten involvement and interest.

I would also throw in some financial incentives. Every school would have a lot of "skin in the game." All schools in the conference would contribute money to a scholarship fund, which would go to the school that won the academic competition.

Winning schools could go on to compete at regional and state levels.

Classes of schools would be set by both enrollment and socioeconomic indicators, so that New Trier, with 2 percent low-income students, would not be competing with East St. Louis, with probably 95 percent low-income students. (Income and educational achievement of parents are the most significant indicators of student achievement.)

> We must do something to increase parental and community interest in academics. Some of the frenzy surrounding Friday night football should be redirected toward learning.
>
> Otherwise, countries that are focused as intently on academics as we are on sports will soon "have us for lunch" in economic terms.
>
> —Jim Nowlan

Higher Education: Entering a Whirlwind of Change

Illinois has a large and diverse system of higher education. The state is home to 9 public universities, 48 community colleges in thirty-nine districts, and 123 private colleges and universities.[39] In the fall of 2012 these institutions enrolled 846,700 students, with a full-time-equivalent enrollment of 625,400.[40] Public universities enrolled 198,400, or 23.4 percent of the total, while community colleges represented 42 percent and independent institutions, 34 percent.

According to the National Student Clearinghouse Research Center, Illinois universities are relatively efficient, at least as measured by college completion rates. For example, in 2011 Illinois public universities graduated 72.7 percent of their students within six years, placing Illinois third among the states, compared to a national average of 60.6 percent.[41]

But according to a 2010 report by the College Board, only 38.1 percent of young adults (persons aged twenty-five to thirty-four) in the state have earned an associate's degree or higher.[42] This places Illinois fourteenth among the states and below the U.S. average of 40.4 percent. This also puts Illinois behind Spain, Australia, and Ireland, with rates of 39 to 44 percent and well behind Canada, Korea, Russia, and Japan, each of which has a completion rate higher than 50 percent.

Following significant increases in state funding during the 1990s, state appropriations for higher education operations declined in the early twenty-first century from $2.418 billion in 2002 to $1.981 billion in 2013.[43] To have maintained the $2.418 billion in purchasing power of 2002, adjusted for inflation, would have required $3.147 billion in 2013, $1 billion more than appropriated. We should note that these figures do not include state funding for higher education retirement plans, which until 2012 had come from a separate appropriation for all five state retirement programs. From 2002 to

2013 annual appropriations for higher education pensions increased from $235 million to $1.253 billion. The recent, dramatic increases in funding for pensions, discussed in chapter 2, tend to crowd out funding for instruction.

For decades, funding increases for K–12 and higher education were somewhat in lockstep, with higher education receiving about a $1 increase for every $2 that went to primary and secondary education. That ratio was abandoned in the 1980s, when pressure to reform K–12 education became a national movement, yet higher education still managed to receive increases almost every year.

Lawmakers and governors are aware that higher education has alternative sources of revenue not available to social service programs, and so it might be able to absorb the decline in state appropriations. Higher education has, for example, revenue from tuition and fees as well as from research grants, and community colleges also have the property tax as a source of revenue.

In order to cope with the decline in funding, public universities increased tuition and fees. At the University of Illinois in Urbana-Champaign, for example, tuition and fees went from $6,748 per year in 2003 to $14,414 in 2012.[44] In contrast, tuition and fees at community colleges are significantly lower, while those at private colleges and universities are higher. In 2011 tuition and fees for full-time students at public community colleges ranged from $2,580 per year at Illinois Eastern Colleges, headquartered in Olney, to $3,930 at Carl Sandburg College in Galesburg. As for private colleges, DePaul University in Chicago would be typical and mid-range at $28,858 for tuition and fees for a full-time student, with the University of Chicago charging the highest tuition among the private colleges, at $41,091. Note that very few, probably fewer than 10 percent, of students at private colleges pay the full "sticker price" because of scholarships provided by the institutions as well as state and federal aid for those who show need.

In part because federal and state grants to needy students have not kept pace with tuition increases, debt for the roughly 50 percent of students who take out loans has increased. For example, in 2008 (the latest year for which figures are available) 10 percent of all students earning bachelor's degrees had more than $39,300 in student loan debt, and 25 percent had more than $24,600 in debt.[45] In addition, parents have been borrowing significant amounts on behalf of children in college. In 2008, 42 percent of such parents borrowed, on average, $30,900 using the federal Parent Loan for Undergraduate Students program.

What does the future of higher education funding in Illinois look like? Because of the tight budget situation for the foreseeable future, as discussed in chapter 2, we predict that state funding for higher education will increase, if at all, at no better than the rate of inflation. Are there any policies that might increase the efficiency of higher education and allow the sector to do more with static resources? We think so.

State funding for higher education is carried out by awarding lump sums to public universities and is not tied to any measures of productivity, such as the percentage of students who graduate in four or five years. For community colleges, a formula based on credit hours produced is utilized.

A different approach to funding higher education was proposed in the late 1980s but dismissed by the legislature. The approach would have routed state appropriations through the students in the form of vouchers rather than to the public universities as lump sum grants, as has traditionally been done. In this way, the student would have more power to choose his or her institution, public, private, or for-profit, based largely on preference. If students were empowered with vouchers based on need, all institutions would, certainly in theory, try to become more efficient in order to keep their tuition low and also offer the most attractive education possible.

Public universities in Illinois chafe under state regulations such as those for procurement of supplies. Directors of complex university laboratories have, for example, different needs and timelines for the purchase of esoteric equipment than do state agencies that often buy in bulk. Since the public universities are largely independent from state government in funding, we think it makes sense to free them from most state regulations and let the market place determine which institutions will be successful or not in the future.

20. Shift public higher education funding from lump sums to universities to higher student aid in the form of vouchers for all students, scaled to need, giving the student more power to select his or her college or university in an open marketplace.

21. In return for less certain funding, free public universities from most state regulation, and let the market determine winners and losers in higher education.

Because of the increases in tuition and the inability of the Illinois Monetary Award Program to fund all students who show need, affordability has become a big issue in higher education. One way to reduce college costs would be to expand programs in which a student spends the first two years at a community college and then is provided automatic enrollment in a four-year college for the final two years. The tuitions of the two institutions could be blended in this "2+2 program," smoothing the annual tuition charge to an average of the lower community college tuition and that of the four-year institution. Another promising idea is the "3+1 program," in which a student spends two years at a community college, then one more year taking courses from a four-year institution offered on the community college campus, followed by a final year at the four-year institution. This would allow the student to live at home for three years and also benefit from lower costs overall.

> 22. Create more "2+2" and "3+1" programs combining community colleges and four-year institutions to make college more affordable.

As noted above, thirty-nine community colleges enroll 322,000 students, accounting for 42 percent of total public college and university enrollments. Many of these colleges have sprawling geographical boundaries. Often the students in one district will actually live closer to the campus of another district, thus making it more convenient to attend an out-of-district college. At present, however, community colleges typically charge students about twice as much for an out-of-district student as for an in-district student (about $200 per credit hour versus half that for the in-district student).

Just as we proposed above that public K–12 school students be allowed to enroll in a district outside the one in which they reside, here we propose that community college students be allowed to enroll at the campus most suitable for them without being charged a penalty for doing so. The "sending" community college district could be required to pay the "receiving" district the difference between the regular tuition and the full cost of educating the student.

> 23. Allow community college students to enroll in whatever college is most suitable for them, at in-district tuition rates, regardless of whether the student lives in that district.

Online Learning

For centuries American higher education has embraced the model of the professor lecturing to a class of students. Today, higher education is adapting rapidly to a new model, that of online education. For example, at the University of Illinois at Springfield in 2012, 61 percent of students took at least one online course; 38 percent of all credits were generated online, and 36 percent of students were enrolled only in online courses.[46] The three-campus University of Illinois offers degrees in one hundred fields of study wholly online. This phenomenon will change the face of higher education forever.

You and your college-age youngster can now take courses online—for free—from professors at the best universities in the world and, soon, we predict, earn college credit for that work. Massive open online courses (MOOCs) are now being offered for free by consortia of schools such as Stanford, Princeton, Illinois, and the Ivy League in a phenomenon that has expanded exponentially in recent years.

"Traditional" online courses are offered to classes of no more than twenty-five students each. They are the same courses as those offered on campus. Tuition is about the same as for on-campus instruction at the public institution, which can be $10,000 or more per year.

The MOOCs are different. They are free and anyone can sign up, which means that scores of thousands have done so, from around the world, for a single course offering. For example, Ray Schroeder is a professor of communications at the University of Illinois at Springfield and a nationally recognized expert on the topic of MOOCs. He offered a MOOC in 2012 titled "Online Learning Today . . . and Tomorrow." More than 2,700 students from seventy countries signed up.

Every Thursday for four weeks he held audio panel discussions with leaders in the field. Students posed questions via Twitter. Discussion groups sometimes formed, as with students of the course in Christchurch, New Zealand, who gathered weekly at a local McDonald's.

The big names in MOOCs are Coursera, edX, and Udacity, all started by professors at gilt-edged universities. They may be superseded by Google and Apple, which are moving rapidly into education. "If they can see a profit in it," observes Schroeder, "you may well see Google U. and Apple U. in the future. Many existing universities would have trouble competing with that."[47]

There are, of course, bugs to be worked out. How will cheating be avoided and course credit authorized, for example? Proctored examinations at testing sites around the world (every community college has a testing site) are now used for online courses and could be utilized by MOOCs. And if a student scores high on a final exam, why not award him or her college credit?

At present, some course providers offer electronic "badges" that represent successful completion of a course. These badges become part of a student's record and may someday replace the old college transcript, which is controlled by the college that awarded the credit. "Free" will become "low cost" at MOOCs in the future, as there are certainly costs involved in providing courses. Google could, of course, sell advertising to offset costs and make a profit.

A MOOC education would certainly be less personal than a traditional college experience, though we recall introductory psychology and economics courses being taught to a thousand or so students at the University of Illinois in Urbana, settings that weren't very personal. But attendance at a bricks-and-mortar college provides its own benefits: experience at living somewhat on one's own, development of social skills, creation of life-long mentoring relationships with professors, and a setting that imposes some discipline on learning.

Maybe in the future some colleges and universities will become affiliates of Google U., providing structure and tutoring to complement MOOCs. Perhaps MOOCs will be blended with traditional coursework.

24. The Illinois Board of Higher Education should evaluate MOOCs as they develop, and where appropriate design strategies for integrating MOOCs into the credit-based programs of Illinois higher education.

In the coming years, K–12 schools and institutions of higher education will have to live creatively with constrained resources. By embracing the best of the online world, educators will be able to reach larger audiences, operate more efficiently and, ideally, more effectively.

CHAPTER 4

Improving Human Services and Health Care

Illinois provides direct social and healthcare services to more than 3.5 million of the state's 12.8 million residents, more than one in four. Specific numbers are unavailable because the state's four major human service and healthcare agencies, and major divisions within agencies as well, are generally incapable of sharing data with one another electronically. This is the case even though there is significant patient overlap because many individuals receive services from two or more agencies and divisions.

The numbers add up quickly. Medicaid is the state-federal program that provides health care for low-income persons as well as for about two-thirds of all residents in Illinois nursing homes.[1] The program serves about 3 million residents in January 2014. Thirty-four thousand persons with disabilities receive in-home services, and 18,800 persons with other, developmental disabilities are also served by the state; 63,000 refugees and immigrants receive outreach and interpretation services. The Department on Aging provides in-home Community Care Program services to 100,000 residents. The Illinois Department of Corrections (not thought of generally as a human services agency) provides comprehensive health care to 49,000 inmates. These are but a few examples.[2]

In 1998 four state agencies were consolidated into the Department of Human Services (DHS); now divisions of DHS, they are responsible for mental health, developmental disabilities, rehabilitation services, and alcohol and substance abuse. The Department of Public Aid was renamed the Department of Health Care and Family Services (HFS) because most of its spending is for medical care and no longer for traditional welfare services, which are now handled by DHS. In addition, there are the Department of Children and Family Services and the Department on Aging. Some would include the important Department of Public Health, although its purpose is largely regulatory and not service-related.

Human services and health care together represent by far the largest slice of the state budget pie. In 2014 the state will spend more than $26 billion in these areas, which is 42 percent of the overall $62 billion state budget.[3] The education of our children and college students, which was the largest slice of the budget before the implementation of Medicaid in 1967, comprises less than 26 percent. Growth in the healthcare and human services sector has been greater than the rate of growth in the Illinois economy. From 2008 to 2014 it grew from $20 billion to more than $26 billion, or about 5 percent per year.

In all the states, much has been changing in the human services and healthcare sectors as governments and local agencies supported by state government try to squeeze more and better services out of budgets that have often been declining; this is certainly so in Illinois. It is hard for us to get our arms around all that is going on. Some of the options we recommend in this chapter are being addressed, sometimes haltingly and with resistance from state agencies, by Illinois state government.

State Government Services over the Decades: An Illustration

There have been dramatic changes over the decades in the manner in which we deliver human services. When Nowlan was a fresh-faced new state legislator in 1969, he was invited to visit the Dixon State School near the city of that name and near Nowlan's district. He explains:

I had traveled on the highway past the school a number of times, always noting the neatly mowed lawn and tree-lined road that led to the school, barely visible, as it was set far off the highway.

This trip was different. The superintendent greeted me on the drive, which fronted a number of red-brick, one-level buildings that looked like college dormitories. Knowing what he was doing, the smiling superintendent led me to Cottage A, which we entered. Inside the door, I was blasted by the stench and noise. Here were 140 youngsters with severe and profound mental disabilities wandering aimlessly around the crowded floor. The place was bedlam. I felt transported back to

Dickensian England, where people were locked up in mental-health prisons and forgotten.

A little boy, dirty and ragged, or so it seemed, grabbed my leg for company. There were only two or three nonprofessional aides for all the youngsters. Play consisted of trying to walk a straight line in this dingy hellhole.

Shell-shocked, I was led out by the superintendent, who took me down a walkway to Cottage C, the same type of building as the first. This time I was greeted by music, bright lights, lots of toys and games, and only forty youngsters, also severely disabled. There were more than a dozen professionally trained staff with the children, if I remember correctly, leading them through games and educational activities such as learning to tie shoelaces.

Why, I cried out, are the other cottages not like this cheerful place? The superintendent, Dave Edelson—I remember his name to this day— responded that it was simply a lack of money. As more money is provided, he told me, more cottages could be transformed from hellholes into well-appointed and professionally staffed settings. But that money was not forthcoming.

Welcome to state government, I said to myself.

Human Services and Healthcare Agencies: Still Operating in "Silos"

A wag once said that "interagency cooperation is an unnatural act among unwilling partners." And so the former human service agencies, now consolidated into the Department of Human Services, still operate in separate silos. That is, the divisions within DHS fail to collaborate extensively and often fail to think first of the client, who is often served by several agencies. For example, a family might be on Medicaid (HFS) and also receiving mental health services (DHS) and SNAP (Supplemental Nutrition Assistance Program), the former food stamp program.

There is not a single intake or registration office for those seeking human services from the State of Illinois. For example, we counted at least nine different geographic office locations in the city of Peoria alone for those seeking human services from the state. According to veteran state representative David Leitch of Peoria, a student of human services, state lawmakers have been pleading with the executive branch since 1998 or earlier to create a single office location to enroll residents for any of the state's human services programs.[4]

The Department of Human Services does have its own model for one-stop intake registration. Based in North Riverside, the Illinois Welcoming Center serves immigrants and refugees in the North Riverside and Melrose Park communities of Cook County. The DHS Web site notes that the center's innovative model "eliminates systemic barriers that immigrants may have in approaching state services." The center helps those who enter with Medicaid, unemployment, rehabilitation, housing, and mental health and substance abuse services, among others. In addition, the Welcoming Center provides referrals to local food pantries, legal assistance, health screenings, and energy assistance, again, among many other referral services.

And it is all in one place.

25. Create one-stop registration (or "intake") offices throughout the state, based on the Welcoming Center model, for persons to contact when in need of any human services or health care.

With state human services offices so fragmented, and with a plethora of nonprofit agencies that serve those in need, the importance of a telephone and Internet-based referral service is critical. This need could be filled by a statewide "211" referral and information service like the one that has existed in metropolitan Atlanta, Georgia, for more than thirty-five years. Initiated and operated by the United Way of Metropolitan Atlanta, the 211 phone service has answered more than four million calls from people who need help or want to give help to others. Many states and metropolitan regions now have 211 services.

Illinois has been slow to develop and expand 211 services in the state. Though work on creating such a system began in the late 1990s, today there are only four pilot sites, serving 27 of 102 counties and not including the metropolitan Chicago region..

26. High priority should be given by the State of Illinois and United Way of Illinois to expand 211 services statewide.

Lack of Interagency Communication

The primary reason why the multiple related human services agencies have failed to collaborate adequately is that they cannot communicate with one another electronically. According to the Taxpayers' Action Board (TAB) report of 2009, Illinois's human service departments have dozens of legacy computer systems (excluding human resources and payroll functions), many of them thirty to forty years old.[5] These antiquated systems inhibit worker productivity, prevent Illinois from reducing costs, and challenge cross-department collaboration. For example, the Division of Mental Health doesn't know if the Division of Rehabilitation Services (located in the same agency) is also providing services to a client of Mental Health!

According to one insider, DHS had more than fifty technology initiatives underway in 2010, which suggests the high degree of fragmentation that exists in the agency's information technology. Reducing the number of systems, standardizing them on a common technology platform, and implementing a unique customer identification system will have numerous benefits beyond information sharing. These include (1) reducing costs by consolidating software licensing fees across divisions and by retiring licenses used by legacy computer systems; (2) requiring a lesser variety and number of technical systems than currently employed across the five departments of the health and human services system, and (3) consolidation of hardware purchasing and server maintenance across departments. (See chapter 7 for further development of this topic.)

> 27. Develop a modern information technology system for human services in which all agencies share information about a "virtual client," who is known to all agencies and divisions within agencies. Since operating budget dollars are extremely tight, use the state's bonding authority to issue bonds for this desperately needed long-term capital investment.

The key challenge in managing human service agencies is the corruption of service delivery by the major interest groups that deal with the agencies, each of which tends to resist change. This is corruption with a small "c," that is, not illegal but instead representative of intrusive oversight by the interest groups, which smother efforts at change that might reduce the revenue going to the interest groups' members.

Tom Johnson was told of a convening of the major interest groups and senior human services agency executives to hear an out-of-state expert talk about changes he would suggest for Illinois agencies. These changes would, among other things, move more Medicaid clients from hospital emergency room care to managed care, where the clients would each have medical gatekeepers to reduce emergency room visits. After the expert finished, the chief lobbyist for a leading health care association stood and declared brazenly, "That is all well and good, but it isn't going to happen, not in Illinois." (The move to managed care is, finally, being implemented by state government, though with resistance from some interest groups.)

The major human service interest groups contribute millions of dollars to state legislative and gubernatorial candidates. These groups include the Illinois Hospital Association, the Illinois State Medical Society (physicians), the several nursing home associations, and the Service Employees International Union (SEIU). These interests tend to focus first on the needs of their sectors, rather than on the needs of the clients and patients. As a result, the state funds not the individual but, rather, the healthcare sectors.

As one state senator observed, "It is easy to put patients in nursing homes but hard to take them out." By that we believe she meant that the nursing home has a vested interest in keeping the resident in the home rather than see that resident transferred to a less intensive and less costly community care setting.

28. Governors must create a firewall between the leading healthcare associations and the management and policy development of the state's healthcare agencies, so that decisions are based on the needs of the individuals served rather than those of the service providers.

Controlling Medicaid Costs

The Medicaid program was created in 1965 as a complement to the Medicare program of health care for seniors and was intended to cover the healthcare costs of those receiving welfare benefits. Medicaid eligibility has been expanded over the years. Today it is a public health insurance program that covers one in four Illinois residents. Medicaid costs are shared between the federal and state governments; in Illinois the split is 50–50. Illinois receives additional federal funding through a complicated state tax on hospitals, and the federal government is providing 90 percent of the funding of new enrollees in Medicaid as a result of the U.S. Affordable Care Act (ACA, or "Obamacare"). Total costs for the Illinois Medicaid program in 2013 were $16 billion, by far the largest single expenditure of state government. In a startling 2013 Medicaid budgetary outlook report, the Illinois Department of Healthcare and Family Services projects that if state appropriations (spending authority) remain flat between 2014 and 2017, the Medicaid program will have $22.7 billion in unpaid bills on hand at the end of 2017.[6]

We note that Illinois pays much more to the federal government in taxes than it receives back in spending in the state. The *Economist* magazine analyzed this topic of state taxes versus federal spending in the respective states for the period 1990–2009 and found that Illinois ranked fourth among the states for having one of the highest ratios of taxes contributed to federal spending received.[7] During the period studied, Illinois contributed $2 trillion in taxes to the federal government and received only $1.3 trillion back in federal funding. The analysis went on to observe that the difference of $700 billion represented 111 percent of Illinois's 2009 gross domestic product.

Federal reimbursement for Medicaid spending is one area where we feel the federal government unfairly shortchanges Illinois. Established in 1965, the Medicaid matching formula based a state's share of federal reimbursement on per capita income. The range of reimbursement ranges from 75 percent of reimbursable costs incurred to a low of 50 percent, which Illinois receives.[8] The states neighboring Illinois have reimbursement rates of about 65 percent. The national average rate for federal reimbursement is 57 percent.

The 1965 formula has been criticized for not considering poverty rates in the states.[9] Thirteen states have lower poverty rates than Illinois, including Iowa and Wisconsin, which have higher federal reimbursement rates than Illinois.

In 1965 Illinois was a wealthier state than it is today relative to the other states. In that year, per capita personal income in the state represented 115 percent of the national average of 100 percent, whereas in 2011 the figure was 105 percent.[10]

If Illinois were reimbursed for Medicaid spending at the national average rate of 57 percent, the state would save about $1 billion annually in its own revenue, which could be spent on education or other pressing needs.

29. The Illinois congressional delegation should pressure the Obama Administration and Congress to develop a Medicaid reimbursement formula that reflects current economic conditions in the states as well as poverty rates.

Six major groups are eligible for Medicaid: low-income seniors, age sixty-five and older; adults with disabilities; children under nineteen; parents and other caretakers of dependent children; pregnant women (half of all births in Illinois in 2013 were paid for by Medicaid); and, as a result of ACA, low-income independent adults. Seniors and adults with disabilities represent only 18 percent of the Medicaid population, yet they incur 54 percent of the costs.[11]

Medicaid costs have been increasing at an average of about 11 percent a year since 1990. Though growth has slowed in recent years, it has been higher than the 2–4 percent average annual increase in the state revenue base. Two fundamental changes need to be made to the Medicaid program if costs are to be constrained in the long term. First, expensive fee-for-service reimbursement and extensive use of emergency room care needs to be replaced by HMO-style managed care. Second, extensive use of expensive long-term nursing home and institutional care needs to be replaced where possible by in-home or community-based care.[12]

Medicaid reimbursements in Illinois are characterized by fees for services rendered rather than by a regular payment to a healthcare organization for the overall care of the whole patient. Fee-for-service payments to family physicians, specialists, and hospitals and for other healthcare services are inefficient and do not serve the patient well. As one healthcare expert (who preferred to be anonymous) said, "The incentive is to do more and we will pay you more, regardless of outcomes." Indeed, there is a disincentive for individual healthcare providers to share and collaborate, because doing so takes time for which they are not reimbursed.

In contrast, the "managed" or "integrated" approach, which provides comprehensive care for a patient in return for an agreed-on regular payment to the providing organization, offers an incentive for the provider to be more efficient and to achieve better and thus generally less expensive outcomes for the patient. And the integrated healthcare provider organization has an incentive for collaboration among the many specialists who take care of different parts of the body and mind.

For this reason, most states have gone to the managed care system for coverage of most of their Medicaid patients. But Illinois has lagged the nation, in large part because of opposition by such major interests as the doctors and the hospitals; these interests prefer the status quo to a system with which they have little or no experience.[13] Indeed, at present the State of Illinois not only reimburses on a fee-for-service basis but in addition makes about $2.5 billion in annual grants to hospitals without any strings attached. As one observer asked, "Is our system about health care or about the economic and jobs maintenance of the providers?"

Only in recent years has the state begun to move significant numbers of patients to managed care. In 2012 the legislature directed HFS to have 50 percent of Medicaid patients in managed care by 2015, but the inside observers with whom we talked doubted that this level could be achieved, again because of resistance by the major healthcare interest groups that slows down change.

In comparison to other states' programs, Illinois Medicaid relies relatively heavily on costly inpatient hospital procedures, laboratory tests, and emergency rooms. For example, in 2006–7 (the latest years for which data are available) inpatient hospital procedures comprised more than 45 percent of Medicare acute care spending in Illinois, compared to the national average of 25 percent.[14]

In order to address the problem of overreliance on emergency room care, in 2007 the HFS launched the primary care case management (PCCM) system, which provides a primary care doctor for children and adults without disabilities. Primary care physicians are paid a small per-member fee each month. About 1.7 million individuals are enrolled in PCCM. This program could be strengthened significantly by tying the monthly fee to specific outcomes that require the physician to actively engage and provide appropriate care to the Medicaid beneficiary.

The HFS must ensure that the PCCM network operates as a true medical home. A medical home provides twenty-four-hour accessibility, much like a hospital or a community health center.

The HFS has been moving an increasing number of Medicaid enrollees to capitated managed care, and as of 2013 about 20 percent were so enrolled. In such a system, the managed care provider negotiates a per member per month (PMPM) contract with the state, which is set according an actuarial assessment of what the predicted costs will be for the covered population of beneficiaries. The managed care company is at risk for any costs above the negotiated PMPM contract, which provides an incentive to keep costs under control and encourages the use of best-practice health, wellness, and prevention strategies to limit unnecessary medical costs for beneficiaries. Other states including North Carolina, Pennsylvania, and Wisconsin have had significant success in implementing broad-based managed care programs.

If used appropriately and coupled with improved primary and preventive care, we believe managed care can provide a substantial cost saving for the Medicaid program, while at the same time ensuring quality of care for the person.

30. Move more Illinois Medicaid participants into managed care programs, in which managed care organizations assume the full risk for medical care; provide beneficiaries with a network of medical providers and monitor health outcomes to ensure quality of care.

The following represent three innovative approaches to reducing the cost of Medicaid. The first discusses the Florida Medicaid program, which allows enrollees to select among as many as eleven managed care programs. The second approach would rely on vouchers with which Medicaid-eligible persons would buy insurance, and the third encourages individuals to take some direct responsibility for their own well-being. We believe all three deserve some experimentation.

Florida's Patient-Centered Approach

Traditional Medicaid places all the patients in the same health plan without regard to their diverse conditions and unique needs. Florida allows Medicaid enrollees to choose among competing private managed care plans. The plans vary with the provider networks and benefit packages. A choice counseling program helps patients select plans that meet their own needs and situations. In 2012 plan providers offered thirty-one customized benefit packages from which to choose. According to one analyst, "Five years after the start of the program, the evidence suggests the program has achieved patient satisfaction better than traditional Medicaid and done so at a cost that is lower and rising at a slower rate than traditional Medicaid."[15]

The Illinois Policy Institute Medicaid Proposal

The Illinois Policy Institute (IPI), a conservative research and advocacy organization, has proposed a dramatic transformation of Medicaid into a voucher program. The approach would allow recipients to buy their own insurance policies and use any funds left over after the purchase as a health savings account from which co-pays and deductibles could be paid.

The IPI believes that the present Medicaid program has failed recipients. "Medicaid recipients wear a scarlet 'M' on their foreheads," declares institute CEO John Tillman.[16] He cites low state reimbursement rates that drive many physicians away from the program, longer waits for services than for the insured, and overall barriers to healthcare access that drive Medicaid recipients to use emergency rooms much more than do the uninsured or the insured.[17]

The IPI proposal would, for example, provide a child under eighteen years of age in a family with income below 50 percent of the poverty level (the poverty level was $19,090 for a family of three in 2012) with a voucher for $3,770. This would be used to buy an insurance policy, which IPI estimates at $1,224, with the remaining $2,546 available for a medical savings account. A child under eighteen whose family is at 100–125 percent of the poverty level would receive $1,885, an amount that is still above the insurance coverage premium of $1,224.

An adult between the ages of fifty-five and sixty-four and below 50 percent of the poverty threshold would receive a voucher of $7,344 to pay for an insurance policy estimated at $3,996, the remainder going into the medical savings account. The adult in that age bracket who is at 100–125 percent of poverty level would receive $3,672, a little below the estimated insurance policy cost of $3,996.

The institute estimates that its program would cost $1.66 billion less in state funds than the present program, a largely fee-for-service system that consumes about $7 billion annually in state funds (exclusive of federal funding).

The IPI proposal has not been enacted anywhere else, to our knowledge. And a waiver from the U.S. Centers for Medicare and Medicaid Services would be required in order to implement the program in Illinois. If the dollar figures estimated by the IPI bear up under close scrutiny from independent analysts, the proposal deserves serious consideration. We should note that in 2013 Iowa and Arkansas applied for federal waivers to allow purchase of insurance plans for some categories of Medicaid-eligible persons.[18]

31. Have the Illinois Departments of Insurance and Health Care and Family Services jointly evaluate the Medicaid insurance voucher proposal by the Illinois Policy Institute and report to the Illinois General Assembly.

32. If the evaluation is positive, seek a waiver from the federal government to conduct a three-year pilot program that would implement the Illinois Policy Institute proposal for turning Medicaid into a voucher program for insurance for Medicaid enrollees.

AFSCME's Preventive Health Care Plan

We believe that costs of Medicaid will not be reduced significantly until the patients are directed to take some responsibility for their own care. A successful model comes from the headquarters of a state labor union. In 2007, Council 31 (Illinois) of the American Federation of State, County, and Municipal Employees (AFSCME) instituted a health improvement plan for council employees.[19] The plan provides two options: signing on to a Personal Health Improvement Prescription (PHIP) or participating in the standard plan. Those participating in a PHIP agree to complete a health risk assessment and undergo common screenings. Participants designate their "main doctor," complete specific learning programs related to their PHIP, and commit to trying to reduce high-risk behaviors such as smoking, being obese, and abusing alcohol.

In addition to the health benefits, another incentive to sign a PHIP is that participants pay significantly less for their health care than do those enrolled in the standard plan. After years of double-digit increases in total claim costs, from 2007 to 2010 monthly claims were 10 percent below 2006 costs.

33. Medicaid patients be required to take responsibility for their own well-being by taking required annual physicals and making efforts

to quit smoking, reduce alcohol consumption, reduce weight, and exercise. The physician assigned to each patient would certify either successful efforts in this regard, which would trigger a small cash reward, or failure to do so, which would impose co-payment requirements on patients for future healthcare.

Other states have negotiated with preferred providers for lower rates for non-emergency surgical procedures. For example, California passed legislation in 1982 allowing Medi-Cal (the California Medicaid program) to negotiate with selected hospitals to compete for Medicaid inpatient services. California obtained a waiver and saved an estimated $300 million per year. Rhode Island is the most recent state to obtain a federal waiver for selective contracting of inpatient and outpatient services. Some states have also explored selective contracting systems that allow for competitive bids from durable medical equipment companies to serve a certain segment of the population.

The *New York Times* reports that a demonstration project begun in 2011 introduced competitive bidding for medical devices and equipment to see if market forces could bring down prices.[20] The results were dramatic, according to the *Times* article. Prices for oxygen equipment fell 41 percent and those for hospital beds declined by 44 percent, among other steep reductions in prices for equipment.

Currently, Illinois Medicaid pays hospitals the lower of their charges or a specific rate that is set by the state. When exploring the issue of hospital inpatient and outpatient services, policy makers should ensure that any successful bid establishes a lower rate than the state would be paying in the absence of such a selective network. We believe that competition, in this regard, may promote lower cost and higher quality.

34. Explore the cost-effectiveness of putting out for competitive bidding certain elective hospital procedures and purchase of durable medical equipment, in areas outside managed care programs.

When Medicaid patients use the emergency room for primary care needs, it not only costs the system more, but also makes the emergency room department less able to serve the needs of truly emergent cases. A managed care system could address the overuse of emergency room care by ensuring adequate, convenient, local primary care access and by establishing a medical home—a primary care physician—for Medicaid participants. Illinois could also adopt additional strategies to decrease emergency room use, to include the following:

- Requiring a co-payment for patients who inappropriately use emergency care.
- Assisting clinics and physicians in supporting off-hour access.
- Providing financial support for the expansion of clinics and physicians' offices in convenient locations, with convenient hours of operation.
- Providing ask-a-nurse phone support to handle questions that do not require physical presence.

35. Reduce reliance on high-cost emergency rooms for primary care through effective, best practice diversion strategies such as those identified above.

Another strategy for reducing emergency room visits would be to work with hospitals to create "Prompt Care" types of non-emergency services as a screen for patients who visit emergency rooms. For large hospitals, this would be significantly less expensive for both the hospital and the state.

36. Establish "Prompt Care" non-emergency clinics at large hospital emergency departments to screen and deflect patients from emergency room visits.

Illinois's long-term care system is marked by an imbalance between the resources devoted to institutional care (nursing facilities, institutions for those with developmental disabilities or mental illness, and psychiatric hospitals) and those devoted to less costly community care options. An AARP report showed that in 2009, Illinois had a rate of older adult institutionalization of 5 per 1,000 compared to the national average of 3.8 per 1,000, a significant difference.[21]

Even the hard-hearted become a little mushy when it comes to caring for seniors who have lost much of their independence. There is a valuable state program called Community Care that helps the elderly live on their own instead of at a nursing home and saves Illinois a lot of money in the process. There has been some discussion of paring it back; we recommend against doing so. When it comes to trimming the beleaguered state budget, we don't hear much about curbing the high cost of caring for the elderly in nursing homes. The state pays about $30,000 per full year per patient for each of the fifty thousand or so who are supported by the Medicaid program for low-income persons (about two thirds of the seventy-five thousand patients in Illinois nursing homes are paid for by Medicaid).

Indeed, we hear quietly about many families who, also quietly, shed the assets of elderly relatives so that they can qualify for government support.

Few families, even those that are relatively well off, can afford for long the $45,000 or more that a typical nursing home charges overall per bed per year.

In 1979 the State of Illinois, on its own initiative, began the Community Care Program (CCP), which seeks to provide limited care at home with the objective of keeping persons out of nursing homes for as long as possible. The CCP provides in-home care for almost one hundred thousand elderly people who can live on their own so long as they have some help with cleaning, personal care, fixing a meal, driving to the doctor, or similar light duties.

The path to the CCP begins with a referral to a contract agency such as Alternatives for the Older Adult in Moline by a hospital, family member, senior housing administrator, or anyone for an individual over sixty who appears to be having problems negotiating life on his or her own. The agency performs a needs assessment in the home of the person in question to determine if she is eligible for long-term care. If the person qualifies for CCP by having less than $17,500 in assets other than her home, car, and personal items, a plan of care is developed for the older person, with a pre-set number of hours of care per week authorized.

Alternatives for the Older Adult then offers the individual in need of care at home a choice of agencies that actually provide such care. In Nowlan's home area, the Henry County Health Department is often selected.

Nowlan visited with several persons in his hometown who receive CCP care. Each was a female, and each was clearly pleased with the caregiver who came in for, say, two hours a day to clean, help the older person bathe, and maybe take her to a doctor's appointment nearby.

Each woman Nowlan visited would be in a nursing home without the home care, from all he could tell, and the caregivers confirmed this. Statewide, we have heard rough estimates that about half of all CCP participants would be in nursing homes without this program. And it is a win-win because the caregiver, generally with experience and maybe a certified nurse assistant's license, earns useful income at $9–10 per hour.

At present, the Illinois Department on Aging (IDOA) serves about one hundred thousand persons through the CCP at an average cost of $10,000 per year (about $1 billion), as opposed to $30,000 to $40,000 in government dollars for nursing home care. There is a possibility that the IDOA plans to limit the program to those who qualify for Medicaid.

Half the costs of CCP recipients in Illinois covered by Medicaid are reimbursed by the federal government. In contrast, the state pays the full cost for CCP participants who have between $2,000 in assets (the Medicaid maximum) and the $17,000 asset maximum for other CCP participants. (Persons with more assets can receive care on a self-paid basis.) Seventy percent of all

CCP participants qualify for Medicaid. The other 30 percent are of modest income but have more assets than Medicaid allows. The CCP is less costly than nursing home care. Thus it makes financial sense to keep persons who do not receive Medicaid in the CCP, even without the federal match.

We are concerned, in this regard, that different eligibility rules for the CCP (in the Department of Aging) and nursing home coverage by Medicaid (through the Department of Healthcare and Family Services) may inadvertently be providing an economic incentive to place persons in nursing homes rather than keep persons in the much less expensive at-home CCP. As noted, the maximum assets allowed for a person in the CCP are $17,000, whereas for a spouse of a person in Medicaid-covered nursing home care the asset maximum that may be retained is $110,000.

37. Maintain the cost-effective Community Care Program even for those of modest wealth who do not quite qualify for Medicaid.

38. The healthcare and human service agencies in Illinois should review eligibility requirements across programs to ensure that the state is not providing incentives to place persons in more expensive settings than is necessary.

There are a number of additional ideas that HFS and the State of Illinois could explore to further its already effective cost-containment efforts. First, HFS could work with other state agencies to explore the idea of developing a first-in-the-nation, statewide government pharmacy purchasing pool that maximizes savings and rebate opportunities for the government by negotiating with drug companies for the best price through supplemental rebates. In this scenario the state would look to pool all prescription drug purchases for which the state is a payer, including those for Medicaid, state employees, state retirees, and the Department of Corrections.

39. Establish a state government–wide pharmacy purchasing pool to increase leverage with pharmaceutical companies in negotiating for the best price through supplemental rebates.

In the 1990s the Illinois Department of Children and Family Services (DCFS) had fifty thousand youngsters in temporary foster care, more than any state in the nation.[22] Most of the youngsters were placed with one of forty-eight private agencies that contracted with the state to care for the children. There were no incentives to find permanent homes for the young people, because the agencies were paid for caring for them as long as they were in the agencies' care.

In 1997 DCFS began issuing performance-based contracts to the foster care agencies with which it worked. Basically, the department said in its contracts that if an agency found permanent, well-qualified placements for 25 percent of the youngsters in its care in one year, DCFS would send the agency more youngsters to care for in the agency's residential facilities. As a result of this incentive-based contracting, DCFS has reduced the numbers of children in temporary residential foster care to fifteen thousand. The contracts also evaluate educational outcomes, family engagement with the children in temporary care, and other qualitative measures. As a result of the performance-based measures, the department has terminated several agencies in recent years.

40. Expand incentive- and performance-based contracting to other human service departments in Illinois.

Certificate of Need (CON) regulations were instituted in 1974 by the federal government. In return for federal funding, each state was required to create a formal approval process before any major capital healthcare projects could begin. The premise was that restraining medical care capacity would also restrain cost growth. In 1987 the federal law was repealed and 14 states discontinued their CON programs, but Illinois did not.

According to professors Robert Kaestner and Anthony Lo Sasso at the University of Illinois in Chicago, the thesis that healthcare costs would be constrained by restricting growth in capacity has never been confirmed.[23] "In fact," say Kaestner and Lo Sasso, "the evidence is clear that allowing market competition to enter a market serves to exert downward pressure on prices."

41. Eliminate the Certificate of Need Program in Illinois.

During the administration of Governor Richard Ogilvie (1969–72) a program of deinstitutionalization began to shift patients from large state institutions to smaller community-based settings. The process continues to this day. For example, as of 2012 there were 1,922 developmentally disabled persons living in five state institutions with between one hundred and six hundred residents in each, at an average cost of $170,000 per patient per year.[24] Most experts in human services believe that clients such as the developmentally disabled and those being transferred out of hospital care fare better in small-group, community-based settings than in large state institutions and nursing homes.

Don Moss is a longtime advocate for the developmentally disabled. Moss notes that care for these patients in small group homes of four to six persons each, run generally by community-based nonprofit organizations, costs from $46,000 to $75,000 per resident annually. Several federal court consent decrees agreed to by agencies under Governor Pat Quinn and his predecessor

Rod Blagojevich have declared that disabled patients living in large institutional settings shall be, if they wish, transferred to small-group homes where the patients might live more independent lives.[25]

42. The process of closing many of the eight state institutions for the developmentally disabled begun in 2012 should continue.

The State of Illinois healthcare and human service agencies tend to operate in silos and have great difficulty sharing data about their clients. Strong gubernatorial leadership is needed to transform the culture of the agencies from that of focusing on agency and division needs to that of collaborative focus on the individual client. By doing so, many of the suggestions put forward in this chapter could more easily be addressed.

Economic Development for Stability

The Illinois economy is struggling. The state's finances are a shambles of debt and unfunded obligations. In April 2013 the state's unemployment rate was 9.3 percent, worst among all the states except Nevada.[1] From the employment peak of November 2000, Illinois lost 655,700 jobs and had regained only 192,000 of those jobs by March 2013.[2] The state's image has been battered by the fact that four of Illinois's past seven governors have served prison time for public corruption or white-collar crime.

"The situation is currently as bad as I have ever seen it," declares veteran economic development professional Steve McClure, referring to the state's environment for building the economy. "I think people should appreciate that businesses in the state don't have to stay here."[3]

"We have to improve, if nothing else, the image of Illinois," says David Vite, former president of the Illinois Retail Merchants Association.[4]

How bad is the situation, and what can be done about it?

Newspapers love rankings and organizations love publicity; this has spawned a number of state-level business climate rankings. As of 2013 Illinois tends to rank near the bottom among the fifty states in many of these analyses, a position that can damage the perceptions that outsiders have of a state, even if the rankings lack merit. Illinois can change those perceptions from negative to positive, but it will take a few years. Below is a listing of some of the more prominent business climate rankings for Illinois, with the "best" state rated number 1.[5] Each has a different focus; some focus on tax burden, and others include broader issues such as public safety and quality of life.

American Legislative Exchange Council (2011)	48
CEO Magazine (2013)	48
Development Counselors International (2011)	48
Forbes (2013)	38
Tax Foundation (2014)	31
CNBC (2013)	37
Small Business and Entrepreneurship Council (2011)	40

These and other business climate rankings have been decried by academics as "conceal(ing) more than they reveal when they conflate a disparate set of industry sectors into a single amorphous snapshot," according to Joseph Cortright and Heike Mayer.[6] Peter Fisher of the University of Iowa agrees, noting that "none of the indices actually do a very good job of measuring what it is they claim to measure, nor do they measure the right things to begin with."[7]

But rankings create perceptions, which are important. In 2011 we took a survey of seventy economic development professionals in Illinois, the professionals who recruit businesses to locate in their communities or regions, to find out what they thought. They reported that perceptions of a poor business climate are important factors they have to contend with in their efforts to sell their communities as places to expand and do business.[8] Three in four of the seventy respondents said that business climate rankings were important, very important, or extremely important, if only for the perceptions they created. Twenty-one of the respondents specifically mentioned perception in their open-ended answers as being important in shaping the initial impressions about a state, and low rankings could often result in quick elimination of a state from consideration by site selectors.

"Whether these rankings are accurate or not they affect 'perceptions' and perceptions greatly influence potential and current business confidence in Illinois," said one of the respondents. "I am constantly having to defend the business climate of our state with existing business," said another, "and it is very difficult to do when every publication you see is ranking Illinois near the bottom of the list."

We asked the Illinois economic development professionals what the state could do to improve its business climate. They responded with these recommendations:

- Reduce workers' compensation liability insurance costs;
- Reduce the corporate income tax rate;
- Put the state's fiscal house in order;
- Provide stability and predictability about the future; and
- Change the perception that Illinois is a corrupt state in which to do business.

Illinois ranked fourth-highest in the country in 2012 in workers' compensation rates for injured workers, at $2.83 per $100 dollars of compensation and 151 percent of the median for the states.[9] Neighboring Iowa ranked thirty-sixth at $1.90 per $100 dollars of compensation, and Indiana was forty-ninth at $1.16.[10]

Florida ranked twenty-ninth at $1.82 per $100 of payroll and, Texas ranked thirty-eighth at $1.60 per $100. This means that an Illinois firm with 100 employees at an average per capita payroll of $50,000 pays $50,500 more annually in workers' compensation insurance premiums than a Florida employer and $61,500 more than a Texas employer.[11]

In 2011 the Illinois legislature made changes to the workers' compensation law, and rates came down 13 percent by 2013, yet more needs to be done.[12] For example, the changes did not alter the causation standard according to which the employer is responsible for the entire medical and disability costs of an injury, even if the workplace contributed absolutely nothing to its cause. All that lawyers for the injured have to do is persuade the arbitrators that the workplace "might have" or "could have been" a contributor to the injury, even if the injury occurred outside the workplace.

This leads to abuse, according to several persons knowledgeable about the workers' compensation process with whom we talked. For example, the Illinois Workers' Compensation Commission awarded nearly $10 million in claims to 389 employees at Menard Correction Center, 230 of whom were guards. The employees claimed that they developed carpal tunnel syndrome as a result of turning the keys in the locks of the inmates' cells.[13]

43. Follow twenty-nine states and enact a law that requires the workplace to be the prevailing or primary cause of an injury before claims are compensable.

Those surveyed also called for reducing the state's corporate income tax rate, which at 9.5 percent is the fourth-highest in the nation. (As noted in chapter 2, most corporations are small, are owner-managed, and generate less than $1 million in annual revenues. The owners often pay themselves bonuses from the profits, if any, so no corporate income tax liability remains. In addition, many corporations are now legally organized so as to pass income through to partners and shareholders.) Although only about one-third of Illinois corporations pay the tax, the rate sticks out like a sore thumb.

In 2001 the economists Claudio Agostini and Soraphol Tulayasathien examined the effects of corporate income taxes on the location of foreign direct investment in the U.S. states. They concluded that for "foreign investors, the corporate tax rate is the most relevant tax in their investment decision."[14] Though the economics literature is mixed with respect to the effects of taxation on business location, William Harden and William Hoyt concluded in 2003, on the basis of an analysis of the literature, that the corporate income tax has the most significant negative impact on the rate of growth of employment among state and local taxes.[15] The 2011 increase in the rate of the corporate income tax generates about $1 billion in additional revenue annually.[16]

44. Reduce the Illinois corporate income tax from 9.5 percent to 7.3 percent, the rate prior to the tax increases of 2011.

State government budget woes also worry business owners. Illinois has more than $120 billion in unpaid bills and unfunded pension and healthcare obligations, more than any state in the nation; this level represents more than $9,000 in debt for every person in Illinois.[17] Business leaders who think about locating in, or moving from, Illinois are concerned that further tax hikes on business may be required in the future to address the massive debt problem facing the state.

A theme that ran through many of the responses to our survey: businesses planning to make long-term commitments in a community and state want the peace of mind of knowing that the political system will stay level-headed and stable for the duration. They want one less thing to worry about.

The issue of predictability and stability for the future was the focus of an April 2013 conference at the Federal Reserve Bank of Chicago about state fiscal policies and economic growth. Northwestern University economist Therese McGuire observed that "evidence is mounting that fiscal policy uncertainty can be harmful to the economy by making businesses cautious to invest, consumers unwilling to make purchases and financial institutions unwilling to lend."[18] McGuire went on to quote 3M executives who had told her several years earlier that "[c]ertainty/predictability in state taxes is much more important in business location and hiring decisions than is the level of state taxes."

In 2013 Governor Pat Quinn proposed raising the Illinois minimum wage to $10 per hour. At $8.25, the state's present minimum wage is about $1 per hour higher than the minimums of all our neighboring states. We doubt that the legislature would raise the state's minimum wage in this context, yet this is just the type of signal of uncertainty that gives concern to out-of-state businesses.

In 1994 Illinois adopted what are commonly referred to as the "sunset laws." Any sales or income tax exemption or credit enacted after that date would automatically expire on the five-year anniversary of its enactment. We believe this provision negatively impacts two cornerstones of a good tax system—predictability and stability.

For example, the state's temporary research and development tax credit of 6.25 percent was re-enacted in 2012 for another five years. Yet business tax departments can only wonder if it will be there after the five-year period expires.

45. Repeal the automatic tax sunset laws and replace them with a permanent joint committee of the General Assembly that would provide ongoing review of our overall state and local tax structure.

Three in four respondents to the survey of economic development professionals also said that perceptions of corruption in Illinois were either "a factor from time to time" or "an important, negative factor" in their efforts to market their areas. "Perception is everything in economic development," observed a respondent. "We are constantly trying to sell a state with a bad business climate and a perception [that] it is being run by dishonest people. A hard sell, to say the least."

Another observed: "Most of our visiting CEOs start our conversation jokingly about the corruption of our ex-governor or ask, 'Do I need to make a contribution to move here?' It's light and not serious, but it doesn't start the dialogue with the right tone." (See chapter 8 for options for increasing integrity in our political system.)

Another hot-button economic development issue that should be mentioned is the right to work (RTW) without being required to join a labor union. Many major Illinois-based manufacturers such as Caterpillar and Boeing have been locating new manufacturing facilities in RTW states, primarily in the South. In recent years neighboring states Indiana and Michigan have also become RTW states.

Three-quarters of respondents to the 2012 annual survey by *Area Development*, a business site and facility planning trade magazine, rated locating in a RTW state as important or very important.[19] Manufacturing plant location specialists McCullom Sweeney Consulting note that 25–50 percent of the firm's clients prefer to make RTW a "pass-fail" criterion. These decisions are generally made prior to any communication with development agencies, so "states are unaware of having been evaluated and cut from consideration because of RTW."[20]

Illinois is almost certain not to enact RTW legislation before 2020. The General Assembly is likely to be dominated by Democrats at least until the state legislative districts are redrawn in 2021. Democrats tend to be supportive of organized labor, which is a fierce opponent of RTW. This only accentuates the importance of enacting business-friendly policies in all other areas discussed in this chapter.

In the 1970s states began to establish business or economic development offices. Generally these offices, as in Illinois, were staffed by bright young people from the governor's office, and some were quite effective. Yet business is about business and government is about, well, government. In order to increase the input of successful businesspeople in a state's economic development efforts, many states have turned to private-public partnerships, with businesspeople appointed to provide their perspectives and assistance.

In 2013, the Illinois legislature created a business advisory committee to help the director of the Illinois Department of Commerce and Economic Opportunity, which is to meet twice a year. The committee's sole responsibility is to oversee the devising of an economic development plan for the state.

In 2005 Indiana established a much more robust way of involving business leaders in that state's economic development activities through the creation of the Indiana Economic Development Corporation (IEDC) and the Indiana Economic Development Foundation. The governor appoints members to and himself chairs the governing board of the corporation, which comprises leading CEOs of major companies as well as heads of smaller entrepreneurial companies.

The IEDC board must approve investments from the Twenty-First-Century Research and Technology Fund, a $40 million fund that invests in new, often technology-oriented ventures. The fund issues loans that can be converted into stock of the new ventures. The IEDC board also must approve any business incentive project deals of more than $3 million that come from the several somewhat typical economic development incentive programs operated by the state Department of Commerce.

Since the governor chairs the quarterly meetings of the IEDC, participation by the business leaders on the board is strong. The related foundation, a 501(c)(3) nonprofit corporation, raises money from private sources, largely from utility companies that benefit directly from new business in the state. The foundation can spend money in ways state government cannot; for example, it can purchase tickets to sporting events and provide other amenities when hosting new business prospects.

According to Eric Shields, policy director for the IEDC, state government leaders are pleased with this private-public partnership, which is free from much state regulation and thus has proved to be nimble and highly responsive to interest from businesses.[21] In addition, the perspectives of the business leaders have been of significant value to the governor in his economic development work as well as that of the state Department of Commerce.

46. Create a true private-public partnership between the Illinois governor and the business community by creating a somewhat independent business development corporation along the lines of the IEDC and its Foundation.

Downtown Chicago versus Metropolitan Chicago

Downtown Chicago is the fastest-growing urban center in the United States, according to a March 2013 edition of *Crain's Chicago Business*. "This is the new economic engine of the metropolitan area and, increasingly, the rest of Illinois," declares Greg Hinz. "And it has reached a critical mass, data suggest, enabling its growth to be self-perpetuating."[22] According to a 2013 report by the Economist Intelligence Unit, Chicago is poised to become the second-most competitive city in the United States by 2025 and one of the most competitive in the world.[23]

Illinois's Factory Floor of the Future

We stood in the center of the factory floor of the future. Behind us was an Intelligentsia coffee shop; to our right were three classrooms and twice as many conference rooms. In front of us was an open space big enough to accommodate 125 digital technology start-up companies and their creative entrepreneurs, each at desks rented for $400 per month.

We were on the twelfth floor of the sprawling Merchandise Mart of Chicago, in the fifty thousand square feet of basically open space that encompasses "1871," a full-service business incubator that cries out, "Collaborate!"

Named for the year Chicago re-created itself following the great fire, the new incubator is built on a scale big enough to generate energy that radiates from the bullpen of desks across to the conference rooms, where ideas are vetted and deals are made to provide financing to move an idea into a business.

Here is what attracted four hundred applications from around the world to space at 1871: talented people, universities, capital, mentoring, and daily programming that brings in successful entrepreneurs and business people—all under one roof. The universities of Chicago and Illinois, among others, a boot camp for entrepreneurs, and a venture capital company have offices at 1871; thirty-six workshops and programs are scheduled for a single month.

When entrepreneurs heard about 1871, they came, from California, Tennessee, Ireland, and elsewhere. There is a lesson here for state and local economic development officials—become a magnet for new ideas rather than a briber, with millions of dollars in tax breaks to keep struggling mature companies in our state. We spoke with some of the people there.

"1871 is a great environment. People want to come here," says Mike McGee, a founder of Code Academy, which provides on-site code writing and Web development training. The for-profit start-up, an idea in 2010, is already a success, having trained 150 code writers at $6,000 per person in three-month immersion teaching programs; demand for their classes is greater than they can meet.

"1871 is unique," says Phillip Leslie, CEO of ProOnGo, a start-up that allows businesspeople to submit travel expense documents via smart phones. "We're stirring a pot of great energy."

Around us at coffee-shop tables, groups of two and three in shorts and tee shirts huddle over their laptops, possibly trying ideas they have shared.

"Trading information is a key to start-ups," says Kevin Willer, CEO of the nonprofit Chicagoland Entrepreneurial Center, which operates 1871. "Our layout, which was designed with ideas from entrepreneurs, encourages sharing and social interaction."

"I was set to move from Nashville to New York City," observes Christopher Jaeger, CEO of Rentstuff.com. "When I heard about 1871, I applied. It's very open. There is palpable energy. We all feed off one another."

"There is now a ton of energy on the Chicago scene," says Leslie. "Four years ago I had trouble finding people I could talk with. At 1871, they are a few feet away. I make contacts with venture capitalists in casual interaction here."

The entrepreneurs who have been accepted at 1871 range from those at the idea stage to those beta-testing (the step prior to commercialization) or operating businesses. Some are on their third or fourth business idea. Once a business grows to ten employees, it must leave 1871 to provide space for others.

Most of the start-ups at 1871, as many as 90 percent, are destined to fail, if history is a guide.

"Entrepreneurs are tolerant of failure, I think," says Leslie. "It's all about learning from possible failure, and then stepping back up to the plate again."

"Our job is to increase the success rate," declares Willer, who adds there is nothing on this size and scale anywhere else. And he has room to expand.

Once a major manufacturing city now known for its financial and business services, Chicago has been behind the curve with regard to digital technologies. With unique adaptations such as 1871, the city may be catching up. As this model shows, the key is to cluster talent and resources, to draw in new ideas like a magnet, rather than prop up yesterday's business model.

At the same time, however, metropolitan Chicago is losing momentum. As Frank Beal, executive director of Metropolis Strategies, a policy think tank, has observed: "Chicagoland is experiencing anemic economic growth, lagging productivity gains, and sluggish job creation."[24]

Economic planning for Illinois is focused on the metropolitan Chicago region, which reaches across three states to include southeastern Wisconsin to the north and northwestern Indiana to the east. In 2011 and 2012, five major economic development plans were produced for the region by World Business Chicago, the Chicago Metropolitan Agency on Planning, Metropolis Strategies, the Chicagoland Chamber of Commerce, and the Metropolitan Planning Council.[25]

The report done for the Chicagoland Chamber of Commerce by the Organization for Economic and Cooperative Development (OECD), headquartered in Paris, France, is the most comprehensive. The OECD used the three-state, fourteen-county Metropolitan Statistical Area as its frame of reference, though it noted that many observers consider the even larger three-state, twenty-one-county Gary-Chicago-Milwaukee corridor a common economic region. The fourteen-county region has 9.5 million people, is the third most populous metropolitan area in the country, and contributed 3.4 percent of the nation's gross domestic product, although it has only 3.1 percent of the nation's population.

All of the reports note that the metropolitan Chicago region has been growing more slowly than most other regions. From 2000 to 2010, for example, metro Chicago ranked fourteenth of the fifteen largest metro regions in its rate of economic growth and in the bottom quintile of all 363 metropolitan areas in the United States. Anchored by the huge Chicagoland economy, the state of Illinois ranked forty-seventh among the fifty states in growth in gross state product.[26] The OECD notes that if the Chicago region had grown at the national rate between 1990 and 2010, the region would have six hundred thousand more jobs than it has today.[27]

Why is this so? While many factors are at play, Beal and his colleagues at Metropolis Strategies lament the hundreds of fragmented, parochial economic development units in Chicagoland. They contend that the uncoordinated, competitive economic development agencies tend only to move jobs around the metropolitan region, rather than create them. For example, the ongoing competition between Chicago and suburban communities for corporate headquarters relocations tends not create new jobs yet costs taxpayers through economic development incentives such as tax increment financing benefits for a relocating company.

"Economic development is too often not about creating jobs but about generating revenues for municipalities," Beal says, as when a city uses tax increment financing dollars to attract a car dealer from a nearby community. Beal believes that the region's one hundred or more economic development units spend $1 billion per year in government funding, workforce training, tax increment financing, and state tax credits, yet have little to show for that huge investment.

And Illinois lawmakers and governors could go further in helping Chicagoland by supporting efforts in the region to give some authority for economic development, and part of the economic development funding mentioned above, to the Chicago Metropolitan Agency for Planning (CMAP) or to World Business Chicago (WBC). If they did so, these agencies could take more leadership in helping the region think as a region, rather than as 100 parochial economic development units and 1,226 separate units of government.

47. Create an economic development unit for metropolitan Chicago with responsibility for marketing our globally influential region to the globe.

According to the 2012 economic development report by World Business Chicago, a City of Chicago unit, "Employers [in metropolitan Chicago] are frustrated and discouraged by the [workforce] provider network in light of past experience and fragmentation."[28] There are twenty-three community colleges and at least eighty-five workforce development providers in the region. Employers express frustration that many of these are more focused on remedial education than on industry- and occupation-specific skills development and credentialing aligned with employer demand.

The OECD report says the many training programs do not communicate well with each other nor with the governments that fund them, "nor—most importantly—with the business community that needs the skills that these training institutions are supposedly supplying. As a result, in the tri-state region, a large disjointed bureaucracy interacts poorly, if at all, with potential employers."[29]

In contrast, southern states such as Louisiana, Georgia, Alabama, and South Carolina have been lauded for state-led free-of-charge, responsive, adaptive workforce training programs. Alabama even constructed a $30 million, 62,000-square-foot Honda training center replete with classrooms and assembly line replicas.[30]

48. Instead of a highly decentralized, indeed, fragmented set of workforce training units, create a state-led program of workforce training, coordinating closely with the Illinois community college system.

49. Align the twenty-three Illinois Workforce Investment Act districts with the thirty-eight community college districts, possibly aligning two college districts with one WIA district.

Relatively few jobs are gained in the Chicagoland region by attracting firms from other parts of the country. From 1992 to 2008, job gains in metro Chicago from relocating firms represented only 2.7 percent of the total. Nearly all new jobs came from hires at existing firms and from new firms created within the region. And job losses from businesses moving out of the area also represented less than 3 percent of the total lost; most were lost through firm closures.

Illinois and Chicagoland lag their peer states and metropolitan regions in new business formation and financing made available to start-up companies. Venture capital firms invested $39 per capita in Illinois in 2010, compared with $76 in the United States as a whole and $141 per capita in peer states.[31]

That is one reason why Frank Beal calls for regional approaches to economic development, in which support would be provided to existing and new firms that cluster around the region's strengths in areas such as logistics, professional services, digital technology, and pharmaceuticals. Beal and his colleagues also call for creation of an Illinois Freight Authority, which would coordinate and help fund the development of a first-class intermodal freight system, which will be critical to the future of our invaluable infrastructure. At present, no government is responsible for freight, yet it is a linchpin of our economy (see chapter 6).

50. Support clustering around the industry groups in which the Chicago region has comparative advantage. This could include subsidies to metropolitan universities to create research centers for the respective clusters as well as creation of an industrial park for a cluster with all the utilities and access features important to that cluster.

Bigger Is Better for City Regions

Basically uninhabited when the borderlines were drawn, states have often created awkward boundaries for their people, or people have organized themselves with little thought for state lines. For example, the OECD sees the Chicago metropolitan region not as an Illinois phenomenon but as a tri-state affair that begins in the north at Milwaukee and runs down into northwest Indiana. Similarly, Illinois as a state is but a piece of the greater Midwest breadbasket.

In *Caught in the Middle: America's Heartland in the Age of Globalism*, Richard Longworth laments the intra-region competition and job poaching at a time when the Midwestern states should be thinking collaboratively about their place in the world.[32] He suggests the Southern Growth Policies Board as a model. A nonpartisan think tank, Southern Growth's research focus encompasses innovation and technology, globalization, and the changing nature of the workforce. Governors in the region chair major advisory councils. Each year Southern Growth releases its Report on the Future of the South, which becomes the centerpiece of the group's annual conference.

Illinois has to stop thinking like a state and instead like a leader in a great Midwestern region whose component communities share and collaborate rather than compete.

At the level of great urban regions, Chicago and Milwaukee similarly need to be pooling resources, intellectual firepower, and marketing skills. Thirty cities in China are larger than Chicago, and one hundred have a larger population than Milwaukee's.[33] In the global economy, says Longworth, size is crucial, and successful cities are getting bigger. Milwaukee and Chicago need to start thinking like the twelve-million-person mega-city they really are. Here again, Longworth calls for governors and mayors across the three-state region to pull together to leverage all available assets just to compete with challengers ten thousand miles away.

In the case of China, governing is simpler. Shanghai, Beijing, and other major city regions operate as the equivalent of "provinces" (states) within China, with few separate governments. In metropolitan Chicago there are 1,226 local governments to contend with. Thus sharing and collaboration are imperative, and Illinois state government must provide the Chicago metro region as well as the whole state with strong planning tools that will encourage sharing and collaboration.

51. Illinois should take the lead in developing a Global Midwest Forum similar to the Southern Growth Policies Board.

52. Governors and mayors of the three-state metropolitan Chicago region should direct their respective regional planning councils to meet regularly, develop cross-state plans, and propose agenda items for regular meetings.

Downstate: Fading Away

Downstate Illinois exists in the shadow of metropolitan Chicago. Like a lumbering ship about to slip beneath the far horizon, Downstate Illinois is fading from the view of our state's urban residents and certainly from the sight of the larger world. Does it matter? Yes, because out of sight is out of mind. Can we do anything to create and burnish a brand for the southern part of Illinois? It is possible.

Downstate is the deep swath of land outside metropolitan Chicago. The northernmost latitude of our state is the same as that of Portsmouth, New Hampshire, while Cairo, 400 miles to the south, is at the same latitude as Portsmouth, Virginia.

There is no statewide planning function, so the large geographic area outside metropolitan Chicago lacks any long-term thinking. In 2011 the Eastern Illinois Development Council at Lakeland College in Mattoon and the University of Illinois Extension Service organized a Downstate Summit that drew several hundred economic developers as well as municipal and county officials. The gathering has been held annually since and may develop into an informal Downstate regional planning and thinking group.

Oil and gas interests have bet more than $200 million on leases on more than a half-million acres in southern Illinois where they plan to drill using the "fracking" method (hydraulic fracturing of underground rock to release oil and gas). For a region with high unemployment and poverty rates, the potential for as many as forty thousand direct and indirect jobs from fracking may be an economic "game changer" for the region, says Steve McClure.[34] This new employment alone would generate from $2 billion to $4 billion in annual compensation. (By way of comparison, Caterpillar employs twenty-three thousand people throughout Illinois). This potential activity alone justifies statewide planning to forecast regional needs for transportation infrastructure, housing, water use, and ancillary economic development potential for the time when the fracking initiative plays out.

From the 1980s until the mid-1990s, the state economic development agency produced an annual economic development plan. In 2013 state representative Carol Sente and state senator Andy Manar sponsored legislation that directs the state Department of Commerce and Economic Opportunity to perform annual statewide economic development planning. We welcome this requirement. In addition, we believe that broader statewide long-term thinking is needed, especially for Downstate Illinois.

When Abraham Lincoln came to the presidency, his base of Springfield, our state capital, loomed large in the nation's consciousness. In the authors' childhood years in the 1950s, Downstate dominated state politics. That was before one-man-one-vote districting and municipal home rule. This meant that Chicago officials had to come hat in hand to plead for Downstate support for legal change in how the city was run.

All that has changed. Downstate now has about one-third of the state's population. The rural parts of that region are really hurting. Rural Illinois has lost 12 percent of its population under the age of forty-four since 2000. Similar areas of neighboring states were also seeing losses, but these were at only half the Illinois rate.[35] Fewer Chicagoans and suburbanites have their parental roots in the Downstate region. When residents of metropolitan Chicago vacation, they most often go to Wisconsin and Michigan. The state lacks a rallying cry. There is no Illinois version of "The Eyes of Texas Are Upon You."

Springfield is really no longer the functioning capital of the state. Governors and other statewide officials, agency directors, and top staffers work primarily at the State of Illinois's Thompson Center in Chicago. The media and the big money needed to run expensive political campaigns are centered in Chicago. The Windy City is home to most statewide elected officials and the two top leaders of the state legislature. Chicago's population has slipped from about half the state total during the World War II era to only one-fifth today, yet it rules the roost in political terms. Any significant change for Downstate must first be approved by Chicagoans.

Chicago has always had a brand known around much of the world. For decades the city has been trying to live down the gangster image of television re-runs. But it *is* known, and now more and more it is known for its world-famous symphony and its cultural venues.

Illinois, which is a kind of default term for Downstate, is not known the world around, not even in its own backyard. A couple of efforts are trying to buck the tide. The highly effective "Adopt a Legislator" program of the Illinois Farm Bureau brings Chicago-area lawmakers into homes and onto farms throughout the state.

And Downstate lawmakers have banded together into caucuses (closed meetings). For example, the House Democratic Downstate caucus of twenty-two members (of seventy-one Democratic members) meets weekly and also often gathers for a mid-week dinner. According to Representative Frank Mautino (D-Spring Valley), the former chair of the caucus and now deputy House majority leader, the four Downstate caucuses (one for each house and each party) have been successful in recent years in forcing the utility company Ameren to provide $1 billion in rate relief to Downstaters. The caucuses have also successfully, thus far, protected that region's 55–45 percent majority split of highway funds with the metropolitan Chicago highway district.

Yet these and other caucus success stories are primarily defensive in nature and are not aimed at building a vision or brand for the region.

Downstate does have some important region-wide strength. The state is rich in agriculture, underground and surface water, and coal (if ever it can be cleaned satisfactorily), oil, and gas. And our network of interstate highways is arguably better than that of any state. Agriculture is doing fine and may become even more important if crops complementary to corn and beans, or crop residue, can be developed into gasoline additives.

What can be done to improve and enhance Downstate's image? The region will never become a worldwide brand. "Illinois" could. Decades ago, the state of Illinois conducted a tourism campaign with the theme "Just outside Chicago there's a place called Illinois." Unfortunately, the campaign was short-lived and never had the impact of branding Downstate Illinois as a destination.

This region needs to organize politically and begin thinking systematically about its future. Otherwise, it will fade from view, like the ship sliding beneath the horizon.

> 53. Ideally, the Downstate political caucuses could join across parties and chambers to develop a positive agenda for Downstate Illinois. This might be based, we think, on agricultural research,

infrastructure enhancement, an improved business climate, and relentless, long-term efforts to promote the name of Illinois.

54. Provide support to the University of Illinois Extension Service to create a Downstate planning and policy unit.

55. Work with the Illinois Department of Commerce and Economic Opportunity to develop a long-term campaign to create a positive brand for Downstate Illinois.

Rochelle, a Dynamic Downstate City

Rochelle, Illinois, is a quiet, neat, city of about ten thousand located seventy-five miles northwest of the Chicago Loop. While many city fathers in the Midwest have been wringing their hands over job loss and stagnation, "Team Rochelle" has, since 2005, generated $1.2 billion in capital investment and more than fifteen hundred new jobs.

"The key[s] to success," declares the city's economic development director, Jason Anderson, are "private-public partnerships" and farsighted local business leaders. Location also helps: the city is at the junction of interstate highways, the intersection of the main lines of two major railroads and—because of the extraordinary efforts of Rochelle leaders—the on-ramp to the fiber-optic grid.

The biggest project for which Rochelle has gained notice is the twelve-hundred-acre Global III intermodal switching yard of the Union Pacific Railroad, finished in 2003. Yet the real engine (if you will) of growth has been creation of the City of Rochelle Short-Line Railroad, whose five miles of track connect business park tenants to the main lines of both the Union Pacific and the Burlington Northern Santa Fe railroads. This "economic development asset" has spurred the development of two industrial parks, generated $1.5 billion worth of capital investment, and created more than one thousand jobs since being constructed in the 1980s.

Rochelle has been aggressive, collaborative, and ahead of the curve. In 1978 business leaders put together the Greater Rochelle Economic Development Corporation (GREDCO), which took options on prime development land. The profitable municipal utility (RMU) became its own Internet service provider, ran fiber-optic lines throughout town, and put up cell towers to give the town, its businesses, and its residents wifi connections years ahead of other communities. The RMU recently completed a joint venture to produce electricity via methane-driven Caterpillar engines at the Rochelle Landfill/Energy Center, which provides nearly five megawatts of power for local customers.

Rochelle also pushed the state to complete a loop of fiber-optic cable out from Chicago to Rockford to Rochelle. Rochelle then looped fiber around the city's boundaries, including 160 acres of land that GREDCO had optioned. This allowed the city to create the Rochelle Business and Technology Park (Tech Park) which is now home to two data and computing centers operated by Fortune 500 companies and the RMU Technology Center (Tech Center).

The utility company leases "server space" in the Tech Center to AT&T, Verizon Business, Above Net, Follett Publishing, and local industries, creating a revenue stream for the city. The facility is designed as a business development center. It provides training rooms equipped with "smart boards" and video conferencing capabilities that are utilized by businesses in the Rochelle area.

Cold storage facilities have liked the dual rail access provided by the City of Rochelle Shortline Railroad, as well as the proximity to Chicago and the stable municipal electric rates. More than twenty million cubic feet of cold storage space has been built in Rochelle to date.

Nippon Sharyo, the world's oldest railroad supply company and a leader in its field, has constructed a $50 million plant in Rochelle that employs more than three hundred people for the purpose of building new high-tech rail cars for the Chicago-area Metra commuter rail service. And Ottawa-based U.S. Silica has launched a new venture called Coated Sand Solutions, which is building a $30 million plant that will resin-coat sand for use in hydraulic fracking. The sand will be distributed throughout North America via Rochelle's rail systems to domestic oil and gas drilling fields where shale deposits hold the promise of reducing America's dependence on foreign oil.

Throughout all this development, partnerships among GREDCO and city, state, and federal agencies have been critical to the creation of jobs and the expansion of industrial park developments. The partners in infrastructure development for the advancement of water, sewer, fiber-optic, rail, and road systems consists of an alphabet soup of government agencies—EDA (Economic Development Administration in the U.S. Department of Commerce), ICC (the Illinois Commerce Commission) DCEO (the state's Department of Commerce and Economic Opportunity) and IDOT/BoR (Illinois Department of Transportation and Bureau of Railroads)—as well as the Lee County Enterprise Zone, Ogle County, and the City of Rochelle.

"One key to solving Illinois's financial crisis is the creation of more private-public partnerships," notes Jason Anderson, who wears two hats as executive director of economic development for both the city and for GREDCO and so is himself a symbol of the private-public partnership.

Rochelle has a lot going for its, but little would have developed without the vision that brought about the creation of a multifaceted logistics hub. Furthermore, Team Rochelle, made up of multiple government agencies, private business leaders, and elected officials, makes economic success a continuing reality in the city.

Water: Illinois's Ace in the Hole?

As many readers wring their hands over an apparently bleak future for Illinois, we may have a long-term ace in the hole—water. We would be wise to manage our great water resources well, while much of the rest of the United States dries up.

Over the course of the past three decades, Illinois has lost a great number of generally white, prosperous, and well-educated residents to the South and the Southwest. But severe water shortage problems are developing there, particularly in the Southwest. The water level in the great artificial reservoir Lake Mead (in southern Nevada, below the Hoover Dam) has been dropping since 1980 and is now near a level at which the federal government will start cutting the amounts of water going to Arizona and Nevada.

Predictive models of the consequences of global warming suggest further parching of the Southwest and the West in the decades to come. And "[c]limate models that predict drying for the Southwest also prophesy wetter times in the upper Midwest," according to William deBuys, author of *A Great Aridness: Climate Change and the Future of the American Southwest.*[36]

Water prices will undoubtedly rise rapidly in drying areas and restrictions on usage may become uncomfortable, even unacceptable. People and business may begin to trickle back to Illinois—if we are ready for them.

"We are still a water-rich state. Come join us," declares H. Allen Wehrmann, retired head of the center for groundwater science at the Prairie Research Institute at the University of Illinois.[37] We have the Great Lakes, which account for 20 percent of the world's fresh water, as well as rivers and aquifers with copious amounts of water.

In 2006 Rod Blagojevich promulgated an executive order that created a statewide water planning program, and the scientists and engineers have projected water demand to 2050. Their work counts three million more people in the metropolitan Chicago area by 2050; nevertheless, the water supplies should be quite adequate if there is good planning and management. The state now has the Illinois Water Inventory Program, yet is has not been funded by the state in recent years.

Lake Michigan provides the drinking water for Chicago and many suburbs, though the amount of draw-down is limited by a U.S. Supreme Court decision from the 1960s. Nevertheless, the amount of Lake Michigan water allocated should be adequate to serve customers until 2050, again so long as responsible conservation and planning measures are implemented.

The suburbs on the outer rim of metropolitan Chicago are not able to hook into Lake Michigan water, so these generally growing suburbs worry about their future sources. Even in their case there should not be any major problems if there is planning for the future that includes conservation as well as the development of additional surface water resources, for instance, the Fox and Kankakee Rivers. Downstate has vast untapped water resources from surface water—think the Mississippi and Illinois Rivers, among others—and from shallow sand and gravel aquifers.

Wars have been fought over water throughout history. The precious nature of water is obvious, except maybe to those of us who take our riches for granted. As Wehrmann observes, "You can't do good planning if you don't know how much water you're using now."

56. Support and fund the statewide water planning work into the future.

Focusing on Fundamental Factors

"Economic developers have reached a turning point," say Steven Koven and Thomas Lyons, "from a focus on attracting firms and toward a new emphasis on attracting the people who can create and sustain businesses with their knowledge and skills."[38] For example, says entrepreneur Aksh Gupta, rather than provide a struggling mature company with $150 million in tax benefits, "Give $30,000 to 5,000 small companies to encourage them to locate in Illinois."[39]

Michigan governor Rick Snyder is shifting economic development incentives in his state from "hunting" for relocating business to "economic garden-ing" at home in support of businesses with the potential to grow. Snyder is using a venture capitalist's approach to state-level economic development.[40] Venture capitalists are in the business of finding promising companies and helping them grow by investing the right amount of money at the right time. Snyder has, in some cases, done away with long-term tax credits and property tax abatements and replaced them with short-term financial assistance.

57. Shift state economic development from a focus on recruiting out-side business to one of recruiting talented people to incubators such as 1871 (see sidebar nearby). Further, provide short-term financial support at critical periods in a business's growth rather than long-term tax credits and abatements.

When a state's business climate is perceived to be poor, businesses in Illinois can hold the state hostage for tax incentives or, the businesses say, they will take great incentive offers from other states and leave. Businesses view taxes simply as a cost of doing business, and anything that can lower costs is good for a company.

States see big business as new jobs, so they offer tax and infrastructure incentives for companies to move. On the defensive, Illinois tries to hold onto companies with incentives of its own. States, including Illinois, are using a good part of their corporate income tax receipts in give-backs and incentives to keep or attract businesses.[41] Until the Illinois business climate improves, targeted incentives, though inefficient, will probably be utilized.

At the conference held at the Federal Reserve Bank of Chicago discussed above, the economist Therese McGuire quoted executives at 3M who ob-served, "Firm-specific tax breaks are viewed as not only unfair but also a signal of a weak, if not desperate, government."[42] According to Koven and Lyons, who base their observations on a survey of economic development studies, "With few exceptions, incentives will not effectively influence firm location decisions. The truly important factors in business location decisions are transportation considerations, labor quality and markets."[43] In order to contribute to an business climate that encourages and attracts entrepreneurs, Koven and Lyons say, the following factors are important:

- Educational resources, especially higher education
- Quality of labor
- Quality of government
- Telecommunications, and
- Quality of life

Illinois is rich in educational resources, quality of labor, and telecommunications. The state's quality of life overall is decent, though the winters can be long and cold. Illinois has faltered in the quality of its government, as has been noted throughout this book. The present governor and future governors, as well as the legislature, will have to work assiduously to straighten out state finances and provide for a stable, predictable fiscal future.

CHAPTER 6

Transportation

Maintaining Our Greatest Strength

Over the course of writing this book, we asked close observers of Illinois about the state's greatest strengths, and our transportation infrastructure was most frequently at the top of the list. Though Illinois has long enjoyed a competitive edge due to its mature and diverse transportation system, that edge cannot be taken for granted as other U.S. hubs and other countries make major investments in their systems. A robust and efficient transportation system is critical if Illinois is to retain and increase its direct jobs in this sector, continue to provide businesses with the access they need to existing and emerging markets, and provide its citizens with mobility to get to work, school, shopping, and recreation.

While the state boasts an extensive transportation network, much of it is old, deteriorated, and congested. Traditional highway user fees, which are a bedrock of road funding at the state and local levels, are for the most part stagnant or declining. Moreover, the five-year capital bonding program, enacted in 2009, is at an end. This chapter discusses these issues and presents some recommendations for dealing with them, most of which call for increased investment.

Current Conditions

The current network includes the following:

- 2,300 miles of interstate highways, more than any states except California and Texas;
- more than sixty mass transit systems ranging from small rural county systems to the nation's second-busiest system in metropolitan Chicago;[1]
- the nation's rail hub in metropolitan Chicago ("upwards of half" of all intermodal freight movement in the nation flow through the Chicago region);[2]
- 77 public airports, including O'Hare, one of the world's busiest;[3] and
- more than 1,000 miles of navigable waterways.[4]

These systems are under the jurisdiction of a variety of entities: federal, state, local, special authority, and private. What the systems also have in common is that much of the publicly owned infrastructure is old and in need of repair and modernization for which current funding is inadequate.

Take the case of state roads. Illinois owns and operates about 16,000 miles of highways, which collectively carry more than 55 percent of the state's traffic.[5] These roads are wearing out two times faster than they are being repaired.[6] The backlog of bad roads on the state highway system is already 2,560 miles, or 25 percent higher than it was in fiscal year 1998.[7] The Illinois Department of Transportation (IDOT) projects that by the end of the 2018 construction program, the backlog will have nearly doubled to 5,047 miles.[8] At that point, about one of every three miles (32 percent) on the state highway system will be in unacceptable condition. Figure 6 shows where the condition of Illinois roads is heading. At the current rate of repair, it will be forty years between repairs on existing roads—and roads are typically designed for a twenty-year life.

Bad roads cost money. They cost motorists money in terms of higher vehicle operating costs—roughly $292 per motorist per year according to TRIP, a national transportation research group.[9] They cost businesses money, driving up the costs of consumer goods and driving down the attractiveness of Illinois as a business location. Finally, when a road repair is deferred, the road's condition worsens. The American Association of State Highway and Transit Officials estimates that $1 spent on repairs while a road is still in "fair" condition can prevent costs of $6 to $14 to later rebuild the same road once it has deteriorated.[10]

FIGURE 6. Miles of bad state roads, FY1998–FY2018

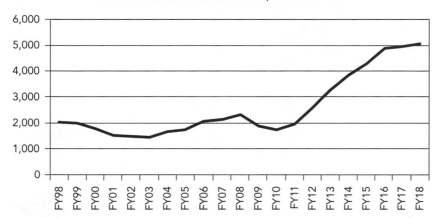

Source: Illinois Department of Transportation, "Transforming Transportation for Tomorrow: Fiscal Year 2013–2018 Proposed Multi-Modal Transportation Improvement Program," Springfield: 2012. Illustration prepared by Linda Wheeler, formerly director of policy and planning, Illinois Department of Transportation.

Although local roads carry less traffic than do state roads, the local systems together comprise more than 124,000 miles and touch the lives of every citizen.[11] A portion of the receipts from the state motor fuel tax (MFT) provide the only ongoing source of state funding for local roads. Whereas road maintenance costs have risen sharply, 2012 MFT receipts distributed to cities, counties, and townships[12] were actually 13 percent less than they were in 2007.[13] These local governments also receive revenues from the local property tax for streets and roads.

Transit in metropolitan Chicago provides far more than 600 million trips per year.[14] The extensive asset base includes more than 1,400 miles of track, 900 bridges and viaducts, 2,300 train cars, and 3,800 buses and vans.[15] Much of the system is old and in unacceptable condition. The Regional Transportation Authority (RTA), the oversight authority for transit in metropolitan Chicago, has identified an annual need to invest $2.5 billion in repairing and maintaining the existing system and eliminating the backlog of deferred repairs,[16] but available funding during the next several years is projected to be less than half that amount.[17]

A healthy Chicago-region transit system is critical to the challenge of reducing highway congestion. In its September 2011 report on the problem, the Texas Transportation Institute (TTI) estimated that congestion in the Chicago area cost more than $8.2 billion in 2010, the third-highest cost in the nation. TTI also estimated that motorists in the area burned nearly 184 million gallons of excess fuel because of it.[18]

Congestion in freight corridors is of particular concern. The TTI study attributed more than $2.3 billion of congestion's $8.2 billion cost to trucks. The Chicago Metropolitan Agency for Planning noted that tonnages carried by truck in the metropolitan area may grow by 70 percent by 2040.[19]

In addition to heavy traffic on roadways, congestion on the railroads is also an issue for the state. Chicago is the nation's busiest rail hub, handling about 37,500 rail cars each day. Unfortunately, Chicago has also been described as "the largest U.S. rail freight chokepoint." In fact, a freight train that takes forty-eight hours to get from Los Angeles to Chicago may take thirty hours traversing the Chicago region.[20]

Finally, airport congestion in Chicago has long been an issue. In order to deal with congestion and delays and allow for future growth, the City of Chicago is in the midst of the O'Hare Modernization Program, a multi-year, multi-billion-dollar program to reconfigure intersecting runways into more modern parallel runways. This work does not involve local or state taxpayer funds. Rather, it is being funded by such traditional methods as passenger facility charges, general airport revenue bonds (typically paid through landing fees), and federal funds. Although state dollars are not involved, continued state support for the project is essential given the 450,000 jobs and $38 billion in economic activity generated by O'Hare.[21]

Illinois's navigable waterways are also an asset, especially for the movement of agricultural products, coal, and other bulk commodities. The operation and maintenance of the waterways is under federal jurisdiction, so in one sense the waterways are not a state issue. However, for shippers in Illinois, the maintenance and modernization of this system is critical, and the state should be joining with shippers to support necessary investments at the federal level.

Modernization and Repairs

In addition to the dismal forecast mentioned above concerning the condition of state roads, the condition of the state's bridges is also expected to deteriorate, with the number of bad bridges projected to rise from the current 607 to 781 at the end of IDOT's 2018 capital program.[22] Exacerbating this problem is the need for replacement of several major bridges such as Interstate 74 across the Mississippi River in the Quad Cities, at an estimated cost that could reach $1 billion. Bridges are particularly critical to commerce, since a bridge posted for less than the legal load limit can necessitate lengthy and expensive detours. Previously IDOT had sought to keep 90 percent of state roads and 93 percent of state bridges in acceptable condition. The 2009 funding package does not allow IDOT to remain anywhere near this standard. Illinois needs to return to that standard so that all areas of the state have roads and bridges in decent condition.

The need for extensive reconstruction and modernization of the interstate system is perhaps the costliest challenge facing Illinois highways, with unfunded needs that will take billions of dollars to address. As a crossroads state, Illinois has one of the most extensive interstate systems in the nation, including three coast-to-coast Interstates and other major north-south and east-west facilities; seven major interstate highways converge in the Chicago region, the most for any region in the nation.[23]

These roads are the workhorses of Illinois's highway system, carrying more than 30 percent of all traffic in the state.[24] In particular, trucks depend on this system, which carries more than 54 percent of the state's truck traffic.[25]

As Illinois's interstate system has aged, much of it is reaching the point at which simple resurfacing will no longer be adequate. Complete reconstruction is needed, and that can be very expensive in urban or congested areas. For example, projects in recent years of reconstructing 8.5 miles of the Dan Ryan Expressway in Chicago cost more than $1 billion, and Downstate, reconstructing 8.3 miles of I-74 in Peoria cost roughly $500 million.[26] The price tag is so high because major reconstructions typically are implemented in heavy traffic conditions and include many improvements to modernize outdated and less safe design features that have been there since the roads were first built.

Reconstructing urban segments, though, is critical, not only for a smoother ride but also for a safer and less congested one. Because of funding constraints, Illinois has not been able to fund any major interstate reconstruction since two projects mentioned above began in the early years of this century. In fact, since 2005, IDOT has only been able to program 150 miles of interstate reconstruction. According to the Transportation for Illinois Coalition, this amounts to only about 20 percent of the miles needing reconstruction, leaving hundreds of miles unfunded.[27]

With truck traffic projected to grow by 48 percent by 2040, Illinois cannot afford to ignore the challenge of rebuilding and modernizing its interstate system.

Continued state funding going to local governments for roads and bridges is provided through a 55.4 percent share of the revenues from Illinois's nineteen-cent-per-gallon motor fuel tax, which is based on the number of gallons used. In the face of higher gasoline prices and improved fuel economy, the amount of MFT receipts going to local governments is in decline. According to a survey conducted by the Illinois Association of County Engineers, between

2000 and 2008 local road construction costs rose by 91 percent, or nine times faster than the MFT distributed to local governments.[28] The local cost-revenue squeeze has been exacerbated by a 2009 statute that opened up local roads to eighty-thousand-pound trucks. The revenue shortfall is so great that in a few instances county engineers have considered returning lightly traveled roads to gravel since funding is inadequate to maintain paved surfaces.

For Downstate transit systems, funding has generally been adequate to keep up with ongoing needs. That is not the case in the Chicago region, which has some of the oldest transit facilities in the country, with extensive unfunded repair needs.

In 2010 the Regional Transportation Authority released the results of a Capital Asset Condition Assessment that estimated the capital needs of current assets. According to that assessment, the ten-year capital needs totaled nearly $25 billion. It included nearly $14 billion to replace assets that were already beyond their useful lives but were still in service. It included nearly $7 billion to replace assets that would reach the end of their useful lives during the ten-year period. Finally, it included almost $ 4 billion to replace or repair asset components so that they could last for their full useful lives. It would cost $2.5 billion per year to fund the repairs noted in this ten-year assessment. Investment at that level has not happened and is not projected to happen. The authority's 2012–16 capital program, adopted in December 2011, totals a little less than $3.9 billion, or less than $800 million per year.[29] Although program levels were more than $1 billion in 2012 and 2013, they drop dramatically in the out-years as the state program ends.

In addition to the need for repairs to the existing system, there are substantial costs associated with enhancing and extending the system to serve new and growing markets. Since 1995, annual transit ridership in metropolitan Chicago has grown by nearly 100 million rides.[30] The RTA's strategic plan, published in 2007, identified enhancement and expansion investments that totaled more than $600 million per year. That amount included more than $200 million for enhancements such as faster service and more seats. It also suggested investing $400 million per year in potential expansions.[31] The authority cannot make inroads on its unfunded repair needs without a great deal of state funding. The RTA oversees the Chicago Transit Agency (CTA), the commuter rail system (Metra), and regional buses (Pace). One-third of the RTA's appointed board members are from Chicago, one-third are from suburban Cook County, and one-third are from the collar counties. The RTA, created more than thirty years ago, has never worked as well as desired, largely because of battles for funding between the CTA and Metra.

Metropolis Strategies, a Chicago-based civic group, has proposed merging the RTA with the Chicago Metropolitan Agency for Planning (CMAP). Metropolis Strategies contends that this move would integrate regional planning efforts because the two agencies now have responsibility for transportation planning. They contend further that the merger would integrate financial planning and eliminate unnecessary bureaucracy. Skeptics counter that the merger simply changes the organization chart without eliminating the inherent conflict between city and suburbs over the allocation of funds for mass transit and commuter rail. We believe that on balance the merger would improve planning and decision making.

58. Merge the Regional Transportation Authority with the Chicago Metropolitan Agency for Planning.

Numerous studies have quantified the dimensions and cost of congestion in metropolitan Chicago. In 2008 the Metropolitan Planning Council estimated the cost of congestion at $7.3 billion per year.[32] The Texas Transportation Institute annually publishes its assessment of congestion around the nation. In 2011, TTI put the annual congestion costs in Chicagoland at $1,153 per auto commuter, the fifth-highest rate among the fifteen largest urban regions in the nation.[33]

Much is being done by transportation officials to deal with congestion in metropolitan Chicago. Some of the activities under way or under consideration include transit rail extensions both in Chicago and in the suburbs, high-occupancy vehicle lanes, bus-on-shoulder riding, and expressway expansions. Mass transit in the Chicago region plays a major role in congestion relief. Without transit, TTI reported, the cost of congestion would increase by 25 percent.[34]

Congestion in freight corridors is of particular concern. The American Transportation Research Institute and Federal Highway Administration cite Illinois as having two of the ten worst truck bottlenecks in the nation.[35]

Rail freight congestion in northeastern Illinois is also acute. Most of Chicago's rail network was laid out more than a century ago, and its patchwork quilt of switching yards, main lines, and connecting tracks was not designed for today's traffic volumes or today's technologies. Without significant upgrades, Chicago stands to lose out as rail traffic (and its associated jobs and economic activity) may be rerouted to less congested gateways. For this reason, in 2003 the CREATE (Chicago Regional Environmental and Transportation Efficiency Program) project was announced. A partnership of the federal and state governments, the City of Chicago, and the railroads, the program has identified seventy projects costing several billion dollars needed to update obsolete rail infrastructure and unsnarl congestion. The improvements include rail-to-rail crossings, rail-highway crossings, improved signalization and equipment modernization. By 2011, sixteen CREATE rail projects had been built or were under construction. The CREATE project office estimates that investments made up to 2011 have reduced delays by an amount significantly greater than would have been the case were the investments not made: a 28 percent reduction in freight rail delay and a 33 percent reduction in passenger delay.[36]

In addition to individual rail and highway improvements, efficient connections among transport modes are also critical. Further, appropriate coordination among the modes can lead to more efficiency in the way shipments are moved. Thus, planning from an overall perspective, rather than a single mode perspective, is necessary.

At present there is no agency at the state or regional level responsible for freight transportation planning and congestion reduction. Metropolis Strategies has proposed creation of an Illinois Freight Authority that would have these responsibilities.

59. Create a freight division within the Illinois Department of Transportation with responsibility for working with transportation planning agencies and rail and trucking interests to mitigate freight congestion.

User Fees and Transportation Infrastructure

Funding to operate, maintain, and construct Illinois's highway system comes from fees imposed on the users of the system. Dedicated user fees have long been the accepted method of road finance at the federal level, in Illinois, and across the nation, for two key reasons. First, they cause the user to pay for the system, in accordance with how much he uses it. Second, a dedicated fee provides the predictability and stability needed to plan, manage, and implement multi-year capital projects efficiently. But revenues from traditional user fees do not grow with the economy; in some cases, they have begun to shrink, posing a serious threat to the continued stability of state highway funding. At nineteen cents per gallon, the MFT generates about $1.2 billion each year and the $99 annual license plate fee produces about $1.4 billion. Together these sums represent most of the $3 billion the state collects from various highway user fees.

Between 2002 and 2012 overall revenue from state highway user fees grew by 13.5 percent, or an average annual rate of less than 1.4 percent, despite several increases in various fees during that timeframe.[37] During the same period, the Consumer Price Index grew by 28 percent, while highway construction costs as measured by the Construction Cost Index compiled by Engineering News Record grew by more than 42 percent.

The MFT was last raised in 1990. Because it is a flat gallonage tax, MFT revenues only rise to the extent gasoline sales increase. Given the rising cost of gasoline in recent years, MFT revenues have actually declined. As higher federal fuel economy standards are implemented, that trend will worsen. Figure 7 shows MFT revenues since 2002. Note that MFT revenues in 2012 were nearly 4 percent less than they were in 2004 and 10 percent less than they were in 2007, their peak year. The Institute on Taxation and Policy calculated Illinois's gas tax rate, adjusted for inflation, between 1927 and 2011 and found that the 2011 rate was the third lowest in Illinois history.[38]

The difficulty of dwindling MFT receipts is not a problem for Illinois alone. It is a problem at the federal level, where highway and transit programs are funded mainly through a flat cents-per-gallon tax. The federal rate has not been raised since 1993 and has lost more than half its purchasing power since that time. It is also a problem for most states, which also depend on flat gallonage fuel taxes.

Revenues from motor vehicle registrations (MVR) also have shown little growth, except when fees are increased, as they were in FY2004 and FY2010. In order for revenues to grow absent a fee increase, the number of registered vehicles must grow. Illinois, with its slow growth in population, is not a high-growth state for MVR revenues. Between FY2002 and FY2012, revenues from this source grew by 22 percent, but most of that growth is due to rate increases.[39] Most of the MVR revenues are deposited in the state's Road Funds, although a substantial portion does go to the Capital Projects Fund, the General Revenue Fund, and various other small state funds.

FIGURE 7. Motor fuel tax revenues, FY 2002–2012 ($ in millions)

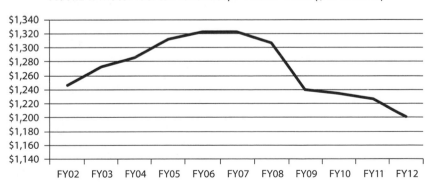

Source: Website of the Office of the Illinois Comptroller (www.ioc.state.il.us; then to Financial Inquiries > Revenues), 2012.

One controversial aspect of user fees is their frequent diversion to purposes other than those for which they were imposed. The Transportation for Illinois Coalition estimates that diversions from 2002 to 2011 totaled more than $6 billion, though they were reduced from a high of $783 million in 2004 to a little less than $500 million in 2011.[40] Regardless of the merits of individual diversions, continued reliance on diverted funds for general, nontransportation purposes does reduce the amount of funding available for highway and bridge work, does weaken the linkage between who pays and who benefits, and does make it more difficult to discuss the need for periodic user fee increases.

> 60. End diversion of transportation-related revenues to general government purposes.

The End of the 2009 Capital Program

In 2009 a major capital program was enacted that provided $9.5 billion in bonds for highways, transit, rail (passenger and freight), and airports. The program also included approximately $6.5 billion in bonds for nontransportation capital projects. It did not provide a new ongoing revenue stream for pay-as-you-go capital projects; hence, IDOT's capital program for highways is projected to go from a high of $4.1 billion in 2010 to less than $1.4 billion in 2016—a drop of nearly two-thirds and the lowest program level since 1999.[41]

For transit funding, the picture is even bleaker. In the 1990s, after a five-year capital program was concluded, the General Assembly enacted small bond authorizations on an annual basis that continued modest state funding assistance until the next major capital program could be enacted. During the first decade of this century, that did not happen. As a result, transit funding zeroed out, and RTA fell farther behind on system deterioration (see figure 8).

These boom-or-bust cycles are hard on funding recipients, who must juggle the timing of investment decisions for capital projects, some of which can take years to move from planning and environmental studies through land acquisition and design, and then to actual construction. Such cycles are particularly hard on the construction industry—resulting in large job losses and leading to business failures during bust time, which in turn translate into less competition (and higher prices) during boom times.

In order to fund the 2009 capital package a number of fees and taxes were increased (including highway user fees), the lottery was enhanced, and video gaming was legalized. Revenue from all these sources is placed in a dedicated Capital Projects Fund whose proceeds can only be used for capital projects.

FIGURE 8. State funding for transit capital, 1999–2011 ($ in millions)

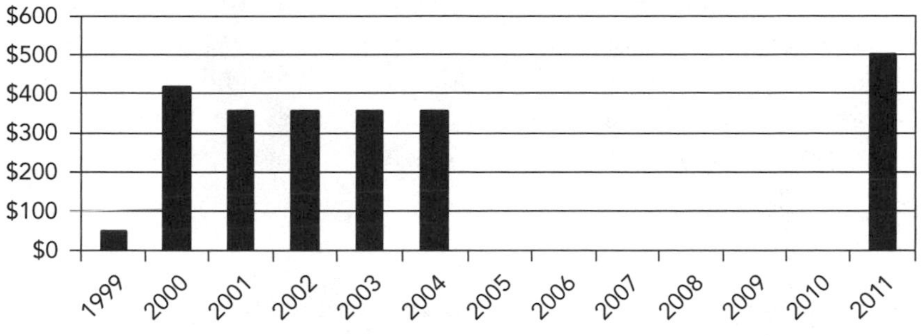

Source: Compiled by Linda Wheeler, formerly director of policy and planning, Illinois Department of Transportation, from appropriations bills for the respective years.

Although there are many benefits to financing capital projects separately from operations via dedicated capital funds, there is a difficulty, too: highway user fees are now commingled with other resources in supporting capital improvements for mass transit, railroads, airports, prisons, schools, and a variety of other state facilities as well as for roads and bridges, severing the linkage between what motorists pay to use the roads and what they receive in benefits. We should note that of the $1.3 billion in revenues deposited in the Capital Projects Fund through the end of FY2012, more than $700 million is from highway user fee increases.[42] The acceptability of highway user fees (and periodic increases in those fees) has always been predicated on the notion of user pays, user benefits. Turning motorist user fees into general capital funding may make it much more difficult to adjust fees in the future.

> 61. Separate capital funding programs into those that are strictly for transportation projects supported by transportation user fees, and another program of capital for all other projects.

State funding for transportation in Illinois is about to reach a cliff as the FY2009 capital package comes to an end. The dialogue about a new state transportation capital funding package should begin now. According to various agencies, transportation infrastructure needs over the next thirty years total $300 billion.[43] As was the case for the 1999 and 2009 packages, any new package should include all modes of transportation: highways, transit, rail and air. There must be a clear statement of overall goals.

The strategic goals of a new funding package need to be discussed and generally accepted. Such goals could include such items as increasing the percentage of assets in acceptable condition, reducing transportation bottlenecks, and providing services to underserved areas of the state. From this agreed set of goals, critical decisions and accountabilities follow: the size of the package and appropriate funding sources, the distribution of funding among various transportation stakeholders, and program targets and projects lists specific to each stakeholder. In order to fund a new package, new revenues are necessary. Taxpayers should not be asked to ante up more dollars without a clear understanding of what the state is trying to achieve.

62. Begin immediately to develop a new, multi-year transportation capital funding program.

There is apparently a turf war being waged politely between the Illinois Department of Transportation and the Chicago Metropolitan Agency for Planning over how to develop and prioritize new transportation projects. Most of the authority resides with IDOT, and CMAP wants a greater role. The latter was formed in 2006 by the consolidation of the region's planning agency and the federally funded Chicago Area Transportation Study group, so CMAP has some transportation expertise.

For its part, CMAP contends that IDOT uses outdated formulas rather than performance-based measures for developing its priorities for modernization activities and new projects. For example, because of an informal yet important agreement in the General Assembly, state transportation funding has for decades been divided, with 55 percent for Downstate and 45 percent going to metropolitan Chicago. This has been the case even though the latter region has grown significantly in population and become more complex and congested over the decades.

The 55–45 split may make sense in 2014, or it may not. Either way, a more rational approach would be to use indicators of the use, condition, and impact of pieces of transportation infrastructure and then develop project scores and priority listings. The authors, admittedly, are not expert in technical transportation matters, but we do think a performance-based approach makes sense. However, any move away from such formulas as the 55–45 Downstate-metropolitan split would ignite a firestorm of political opposition from Downstate elected officials, who would see their huge geographical area as being threatened by the much more populous metropolitan region. Nevertheless, we feel it is time to move toward performance-based measures with local input for developing transportation project priorities.

63. Enact legislation introduced in 2013 that would create a technical advisory group at IDOT that would develop performance measures for all future infrastructure projects, with input from local planning groups such as CMAP.

Paying for Transportation Infrastructure

Most agree with the suggestions of the National Transportation Policy and Revenue Study Commission: for interim relief, raise motor fuel tax rates by some amount, and index the new rate to some measure of inflation (for instance, an annual adjustment based on the Consumer Price Index). The past two capital packages, those of 1999 and 2009, increased other broad-based user fees rather than raising MFT rates. The 2009 capital package has been funded by a mix of revenue sources that included non-user fee revenues, one of which is a new video gaming tax, which has not lived up to expectations. Although the state's MFT rate is fairly low in comparison to those of other states (Illinois is tied with Michigan for 33rd lowest)[44] and though rates have not been adjusted since 1991, MFT increases pose three special difficulties.

First, high gas prices make it difficult to raise MFT rates. Second, gas stations on Illinois's border fear loss of business due to lower gas taxes in Missouri and Indiana. Finally, although basic MFT rates are relatively low in Illinois, other state and local taxes are imposed on fuel. In Chicago, the taxes levied on motor fuel are among the highest in the nation and include a 6.25 percent state-collected sales tax (5 percent going to the state and 1.25 percent to local governments), a 3.4 percent sales tax (various home rule taxes), 6 cents per gallon imposed by Cook County, and 5 cents per gallon imposed by Chicago. Only one of these taxes is dedicated to transportation—the 1.25 percent RTA sales tax, which goes to fund transit in metropolitan Chicago. Despite these issues, it is past time to raise MFT rates in Illinois.

Although Illinois's motor vehicle registration (MVR) rates have risen from $48 in 1998 to $99 in 2012, additional increases or adjustments could be considered. For example, some neighboring states base MVR rates on the value of the vehicle, and some keep MVR rates low but impose property taxes or other fees that bring the effective MVR rate to a much higher level. (Value-based taxes on personal property are prohibited by the Illinois Constitution.) At one time, Illinois varied its rate, with larger cars paying higher fees. At the 2012 rate of $99, there is still room to consider higher fees or some adjustments to the ways fees are imposed. The strength of MVR fees is that they are a broad-based revenue source, generating substantial amounts of income. The downside is that they have very little growth. It may now be desirable to build a modest growth rate into MVR revenues.

64. Base MVR rates on the value of the vehicle.

In addition to the broad-based revenue sources, there are other new revenue sources and financing options to consider. We discuss some of these below.

Fees on Vehicle Miles Traveled

We should begin immediately to lay the groundwork for replacing the MFT with some form of fee based on vehicle miles traveled (VMT). These fees could be determined by annual inspection of odometers or possibly by on-board computers with global positioning satellite (GPS) capability. Advances in technology offer new possibilities for assessing and collecting such fees while still protecting the privacy of motorists.

In 2007 the Oregon Department of Transportation reported on a successful pilot program in which motorists were taxed "at the pump" via GPS connection to devices onboard the automobiles that recorded miles traveled, and for which the motorists were taxed on their fuel bill. Report authors stated, "The pilot program showed that, using existing technology in new ways, a mileage fee could be implemented to replace the gas tax as the principal revenue source for road funding."[45]

Additional Tolling

Tolling has been highly successful in Illinois, bringing the state the benefits of 295 miles of high-capacity roadways that serve 8.6 billion vehicle miles of travel each year.[46] Since 2000 most new expressways in northeastern Illinois have been constructed as tollways; that trend should continue, and several new tollways are in the planning stages. Before the federal highway funding program called MAP-21 was renewed in 2012, there were federal restrictions on converting free interstates to toll roads. The federal program eased up slightly on these restrictions, allowing tolls on new lanes as long as the same number of free lanes is maintained.

Tolls continue to be a vital source for adding high-capacity facilities to metropolitan Chicago, but their applicability elsewhere in Illinois is currently very limited. At one time, there were discussions about using tolls for the new bridge between southwest Illinois and St. Louis, but that would have required tolling all bridges in the metro area to keep traffic from diverting from the tolled facility. The idea was dropped. Traffic levels in Downstate are not considered high enough to completely fund new facilities via tolls alone; in fact, even in northeast Illinois construction of new toll roads is typically subsidized in the early years by revenues from the existing toll road system to keep tolls at a reasonable level.

Congestion Pricing

With congestion pricing, tolls (often variable) are placed on one or more expressway lanes that provide a free-flow ride while adjacent lanes remain free (or tolled at a lower rate) and move more slowly. Such lanes are in place in several major metropolitan areas, but there are none in Chicagoland, although there has been much discussion and study of this option. It seems likely that congestion pricing will (and should) be applied to some portion of Chicago's congested expressways. Because strong mass transit ridership directly benefits drivers on congested roadways, revenues from congestion pricing could be an ideal dedicated funding source for metropolitan Chicago transit improvements.

Fees on Shipping

Shipping fees are often mentioned as a potential funding source for freightway improvements. The Alameda Corridor improvements in California, for instance, were funded in part by a fee on all containers passing through the ports of Los Angeles and Long Beach. Such fees are not mode-driven, so they might offer opportunities for projects that involve more than one mode. One issue with such fees is the extent to which projects funded in this manner might be perceived to benefit one mode or one company more than another. If such a fee were imposed, it would be critical to set up an equitable process for project selection among competing private-sector stakeholders.

Public-Private Partnerships

Since public funds for transportation projects have been inadequate to maintain and develop our transportation systems in Illinois, the state should rather aggressively evaluate the potential for public-private partnerships (referred to as P3s) that would infuse major projects with private-sector money. The states have not generally made much use of the P3s, which are basically projects in which private investors share in the funding of public projects and also benefit from a stream of revenue from the projects in order to pay back investors. Tollways would be examples of projects with clear investment and revenue stream flows.

Such P3s are used much more extensively in Canada and Europe than in the United States, although Virginia and Texas have significant experience with P3s for transportation projects. Sometimes P3s make sense; sometime they don't. "The keys to a successful public-private partnership are having a public sector leader/champion, solid statutory foundation, dedicated PPP team from the public sector, detailed business plan, clearly defined revenue stream, complete stakeholder support, and careful vetting of the private partners," says Richard Norment, executive director of the National Council for Public-Private Partnerships. "If any one of these is missing there is a higher potential for failure in the project."[47]

65. Generate increased revenues for transportation infrastructure investments from some mix of the above revenue options.

Airport Expansion

O'Hare International Airport, one of the busiest airports in the world, has long suffered from serious delays, but that is improving as the City of Chicago continues to move forward with its multibillion-dollar plan to reconfigure O'Hare. Several major projects have already been completed and others are in design and planning. Completing this critical work will bring substantial economic benefits to the state. Although state funding is not needed for completing the transformation, the state should continue to be a strong supporter of the O'Hare master plan.

In tandem with O'Hare redevelopment, the state has long pursued planning for the South Suburban Airport, a supplemental air carrier airport in Will County. It is still in the planning stages. However, the state has been purchasing land to preserve the site for eventual construction. The next state capital package should continue the funding necessary for ongoing land acquisition. In addition, the state should work with local governments and other stakeholders to establish an airport authority to guide this project.

66. Complete the O'Hare reconfiguration; continue planning for the South Suburban Airport.

Intercity Rail Reliability

Chicago is the Midwest hub for intercity passenger rail service, with fifty-six trains per day.[48] In federal FY2012, these trains served more than 5 million riders at thirty Illinois stations, including Chicago, the fourth-busiest station in the Amtrak system.[49] Ridership has been growing: the FY2012 figure represents a 4 percent increase from the previous year.[50] Although most of this service is funded at the federal level, Illinois supplements this service with funding for additional trains on corridors from Chicago to St. Louis, to Quincy, and to Carbondale. Moreover, Illinois and Wisconsin jointly subsidize additional trains on the Chicago-Milwaukee corridor. These services are valued assets to the communities they serve. As the state considers future intercity rail passenger investments, certain principles should apply.

Currently the state is spending $1.5 billion to develop 110 mile-per-hour service on the St. Louis–Chicago corridor.[51] This money is going for new rolling stock and locomotives as well as track and signal improvements between Joliet and Alton. None of it is going to reduce major bottlenecks that exist between Alton and St. Louis and between Joliet and Chicago. These bottlenecks, which today seriously impede on-time performance, are likely to worsen as rail freight traffic grows. For many travelers, particularly business travelers, a top speed of 110 mph is probably less compelling than on-time service. Reliability of intercity rail passenger service should be the premier goal guiding investment decisions.

The $1.5 billion being expended for high-speed rail in Illinois provides a single track, with sidings, along the corridor. It would take $4.2 billion to $5 billion more to add a second track as well as to eliminate bottlenecks at the St. Louis and Chicago ends of the line.[52] The goal is to reduce travel times between Chicago and St. Louis by fifty minutes or more from the current time of nearly five and one-half hours (the current project for $1.5 billion)[53] and ultimately to reduce it to just under four hours (the full-build project for another $4.2 billion to $5 billion).[54] That is a significant reduction in travel times, but if the second investment is not made, the benefits could be greatly diminished because of bottlenecks at both ends of the line. If the full-build project moves forward, it will require unprecedented resources for a single Illinois rail corridor.

Current annual ridership on the corridor in 2012 was 650,000; it is projected to rise to 1.1 million with the current $1.5 billion investment.[55] With the additional $4.2 billion to $5 billion investment, projected ridership would rise to an estimated 1.7 million.[56] By contrast, RTA carries 2 million riders on an average weekday.[57] Given the state's bleak financial picture and the number of beneficiaries, there are legitimate questions about whether this level of investment is the best use of scarce resources. On the other hand, the current funding for high-speed rail consists mostly of federal funds, so it could be considered "free money." Nonetheless, decisions about future major investments in high-speed rail should consider whether the cost is proportionate to the benefits projected.

The operating subsidy for state-sponsored rail service used to come from the General Revenue Fund. Beginning with FY2012, the $26 million annual subsidy was shifted to the Road Fund. The high-speed rail service will push these subsidies higher because of the higher frequency of train service on the corridor and the need to reimburse the freight railroad that owns the corridor for the cost of maintaining the corridor to higher standards than those needed for freight service. Further, Illinois is constructing improvements to initiate rail passenger service in two new corridors, from Chicago to Rockford and Dubuque and from Chicago to the Quad Cities. These new services will also require additional operating subsidies. There has been little to no public discussion of the additional operating and maintenance costs associated with these capital investments. As future rail investments are considered, the decisionmaking process needs to publicly disclose how much additional operating subsidy will be required and how it is to be funded.

67. For passenger rail, make reliability a higher priority than speed.

Conclusion

There are many other transportation issues, but three are critical. First, provide the funding to stem the slide into infrastructure disrepair, especially for roads, bridges, and metropolitan Chicago's transit. Second, develop alternatives for supplementing or replacing dwindling MFT revenues. Third, address congestion, particularly in the freight sector, so that Illinois can handle in a more cost-effective way today's freight volumes and the robust growth that is projected to occur—either in Illinois, or elsewhere if the state is not ready. These are economic make-or-break issues for Illinois.

Reengineering Our Governments

As noted in chapter 2, even if Illinois maintains the income tax increases of 2011, the state is still projected to run a deficit of about $2 billion per year, according to the respected Institute of Government and Public Affairs at the University of Illinois. Simply to reduce spending on what we do at present will not be sufficient. In addition, we need to rethink how we do what we need to do. In this chapter, we take a look at several management challenges facing Illinois. Although this account is not exhaustive, we hope the illustrations that follow will spark interest in further evaluation of our state and local government structures and operations.

Information Technology Needs

We have spoken in this work of the need for long-term thinking and planning in Illinois. Yet this requires good information, and in this regard, Illinois state government is sorely deficient. Information technology serves basically two categories of government functions: financial management and operations, which we take in order.

The state's auditor general found in 2011 that state agencies reported using 263 different decentralized financial reporting systems.[1] (A former consultant to Illinois state government, who asked not to be named, said there are actually more than 1,000 separate accounting systems, often one each for small programs within agencies.) More than half of the reporting systems cannot communicate with others, requiring manual intervention to convert data from one system to another. One result is that the Illinois Comprehensive Annual Financial Report takes more than a year following the end of a fiscal year to complete, whereas other states can finish their reports in sixty to ninety days.

68. Replace the multitudinous financial reporting systems with a single entity-wide accounting system.

69. Enact a statute that directs the governor to provide quarterly reports on the financial condition of the state on the basis of Generally Accepted Accounting Principles (GAAP). This would require the governor to implement a uniform system of statewide accounting using modern digital processing for the state's financial activities. This would also make it possible to issue the important Comprehensive Annual Financial Report in a timely manner.

It takes days or weeks from the time a state agency receives funds until the time those funds are available for expenditure. The current practice is for an agency to deliver a notice to the state treasurer that funds have been deposited in an account. The treasurer issues a nonnegotiable draft and sends it to the agency; the agency completes a form that identifies the appropriate account for the funds and sends the form, often weekly, to the state comptroller, along with the nonnegotiable drafts. The comptroller then notifies the treasurer that the funds are available for expenditure. The funds are invested as soon as they are received.

If this paper-intensive process could be automated, the annual and one-time benefits would be substantial. Transaction costs that include personnel, paper, postage, courier fees, and overhead could be reduced. In addition, the one-time benefit of processing receipts more quickly is significant. Fred Montgomery, an accountant and board member of the Taxpayers' Federation of Illinois, explains:

"Let's assume the State will receive $200 million per week, every week, forever, beginning a week from tomorrow. (This is like saying the that the automation of the cash accounting process will affect $10 billion within one year, that the state will continue to receive the $10 billion [at least] forever, and that the automation will reduce the cash accounting process by an average of seven days.) Now, instead of receiving $200 million per week, every week, forever beginning a week from tomorrow, let's assume that the State receives the first $200 million today—seven days early—because it has automated its cash accounting process. Since the cash will be received forever, the State has an additional $200 million today and its weekly revenues in the future will not be any less, so this is the 'permanent savings'—actually it's a 'permanent benefit.' This is not additional income because no one has to pay any amount more than they otherwise would, and the State's revenues are not any higher than they otherwise would be. It's simply that the cash is available to be spent sooner.

"The practice of accelerating the availability of cash is very common in the business world. However, it is not easily understood by those who are not familiar with corporate finance and accounting. I think this is one of the main reasons that people in some governments have not pushed for more automation of the cash accounting process."[2]

> 70. Create an automated cash accounting system in Illinois state gov-
> ernment.

In his 2011 report on the state's financial reporting system, the auditor general noted that Illinois operates with an "estimated 900 funds."[3] In contrast, Michigan operates with only 76 funds, and Wisconsin with 60. The auditor general noted that "[f]inancial transactions accounted for in a complex fund structure increase the risk for errors and omissions, increase the level of effort necessary to account for and report transactions, and complicate the combining process for financial reporting in accordance with GAAP (Generally Accepted Accounting Principles). Additionally, numerous transfers among funds hinder useful financial analysis. The risk of financial reporting errors is also increased when financial activity includes numerous transfers among funds."[4] He goes on to recommend that the "Governor's Office and the Office of the Comptroller . . . work with the General Assembly to reduce the complexity of the State's fund structure."[5]

> 71. Reduce the number of funds with which state government oper-
> ates.

The lack of modern information technology also fosters highly inefficient operations within and across state agencies. We provide two brief examples, one from the Illinois Department of Corrections (IDOC) and the other from the several human services agencies.

With eleven thousand employees, IDOC is one of state government's largest employers. Yet the prison guards still fill out manual time-keeping sheets. Worse, the department cannot communicate electronically with Cook County corrections officials nor with the parole officers who oversee released inmates. For example, an insider told us that a Cook County Jail inmate tested for AIDS who is sent to the Illinois Department of Corrections has to be tested again because of poor communication between the agencies.

Further, the IDOC systems that track offenders and parolees, respectively, are not linked. As a result, movement of an offender from incarceration to parole cannot be shared by the systems electronically. Further, case management data cannot be stored for more than two years, despite the need to keep case data for a longer period. Old computer workstations are extremely slow, with log-on times taking upwards of thirty minutes. There are other severe information technology, telecommunications, and radio infrastructure problems that require a major overhaul and modernization.

Progress is being made at IDOC. According to department communications director Tom Shaer, "The agency is well into a program of completely replacing its information technology. The goal is to have the 32-year-old mainframe computer gone by the first quarter of 2014."[6]

More troubling, the human services agencies' computer systems, and even those of divisions within the Department of Human Services, are unable to communicate with one another. There is no master client identifier that would tell what services a client receives from which agencies. This makes it almost impossible for case workers to follow clients in a holistic manner.

To this point, however, modernization of information technologies in state government has been budgeted, or not, in the annual operating budgets of the individual agencies. In times of constrained budgets, which are persistent in Illinois, investment in new technology competes with current operating costs, and technology loses out. The result is an antiquated, fragmented hodge-podge of information technology programs.

72. Make a major investment in a comprehensive modernization and standardization of information technologies for Illinois state government that would allow for the following:

- Centralized financial reporting that would be more timely and transparent than the present decentralized system;
- Integrated management of human services client information; and
- "Big data" analysis of huge information sets that could connect data from various state agencies.

Instead of trying, futilely, to finance this modernization through individual agency operating budgets, we suggest that these expensive upgrades, which could cost scores of millions of dollars, be funded through the capital budget, which funds long-term investment projects. This is the only way the absolutely necessary project will ever be accomplished.

73. Finance information technology reengineering with long-term capital fund bond borrowing.

Information technology (IT) is now such a critical function of state government that it needs a visible home. There is at present a chief information officer. But he has neither staff nor authority. Some of the IT functions of the state are handled by the Department of Central Management Services and some by the individual agencies. Nobody is in charge.

The State of Illinois needs a separate department for IT, headed by someone with the position of chief information officer. This department would be responsible for long-term IT planning, capital investment decision making for IT, the outsourcing of state IT services, and sharing of services with interested local governments.

74. Create a Department of Information Technology for the State of Illinois, headed by the state's chief information officer.

Note that efforts to improve the state's IT have been initiated by the administration of Governor Pat Quinn. The governor's Office of Management and Budget issued a request for proposals for a five- to ten-year contract for a consultant to help oversee a major modernization of information technology across the agencies of the governor.[7]

State Personnel System

Rod Blagojevich, governor from 2003 to 2009, nearly destroyed the state personnel system. The process limps along, dominated by unions, stripped of many of its experienced middle- and upper-rung professionals, lacking management tools to reward and sanction, and unattractive to the next generation of capable employees. This is Blagojevich's most serious crime against Illinois. It will take a generation to restore what has been lost, according to insiders. When the authors were directors of several state agencies during the early 1980s, the state personnel system comprised three layers:

- a top layer of political and professional employees in policymaking positions, who could be dismissed at any time;
- a deep middle layer of employees protected by the civil service system and rewarded by a merit compensation program, and third,
- a level of generally low-skill employees, difficult to differentiate by civil service examination, who were protected by union membership.

Today, we have a dysfunctional system in which the middle layer has basically vanished and the top layer is basically protected from dismissal at will by union protection.

State government staffing has been reduced dramatically since 2003. An early retirement program accompanied Blagojevich into office in 2003, when thousands took advantage of the program, reducing state employment rolls from 87,420 in 2002 to 75,250 in 2004. Since then overall state employment has declined further, to 64,328 in 2012, according to the Office of the Comptroller.[8] Robert Powers was deputy general counsel for personnel for Governor George Ryan from 1999 to 2003, the years immediately preceding the governorship of Rod Blagojevich. He observes that "Blagojevich took over the Civil Service Commission, created hundreds of Rutan exempt positions (positions exempt from prohibitions on political hiring), put his own people into the jobs, then protected them by making the relatively high-level positions part of the union contract."[9]

Blagojevich demeaned state employees publicly and struck fear into the hearts of many upper-level state employees, who worried that they would be the next to be fired. Paranoia developed from the top ranks on down about who was going to be forced out to make room for often incompetent Blagojevich hires. As a result, many veteran, highly competent employees retired or left state employment during the early years of the Blagojevich administration.

A confidential legislative staff analysis conducted in 2013 stated that 96 percent of all state employees under the governor now belong to a union, and the figure may reach 99 percent once the outcome of pending union certification requests is known. Senior executives have often joined unions, primarily the American Federation of State County and Municipal Employees (AFSCME). Their reasons are understandable. After the year 2000, union members benefited from pay increases totaling 36 percent (about 50 percent if we include longevity "step" increases and compounding), as a result of very attractive collective bargaining contracts. At the same time, non-union management and supervisory employees actually received pay cuts because of a pay freeze plus required unpaid furlough days.

As a result, union members now often supervise union members, which is awkward and ineffective because union supervisors are often reluctant to discipline fellow union members. "Almost all SPSAs [senior public service administrators, the elite of the public service] have gone union," observes another friend who works in state government.

Today, fewer than two thousand employees are in the ranks of those who work on a merit compensation basis, and many of them make much less money than do the union employees they supervise. Understandably, union employees capable of moving into non-union management posts are generally unwilling to leave the safety of their union roles to take more senior positions. An inside employee who wished to remain anonymous told us that there are forty-seven or more Illinois state government worksites where there are no non-union supervisory employees present. (In 2013 Governor Quinn and legislative leaders enacted legislation that authorizes the governor to "exclude a specified number of State employment positions from the self-organization and collective bargaining provisions of the [Illinois Labor Relations] Act." According to the governor's press office, as of 2013, "We have filed to decertify 160 positions and are in the process of filing 1,350 more.")

The work attitude is "to hell with it," says one merit compensation employee, once a loyal and highly professional manager. "I leave right at 4:30 now, and that's not the way it should be." Another management employee complains that under Blagojevich senior management ranks swelled to provide jobs for friends, while the number of employees who delivered front-line services was cut back. "We used to have a director and one deputy director at our agency," our friend said. "Now we have so many deputy directors they are tripping over one another."

We believe that public employee unions have too much influence over the management of state agencies. For example, the unions have ingrained into collective bargaining agreements their fetish for promotion on the basis of seniority rather than merit. As a result, state government executives and managers have lost their capacity to reward and sanction their employees. One non-union manager we know reported, for example, that he tried to promote a deserving employee to a better job, but because of required union posting of job openings and seniority, the wrong person got the job. We are confident that this is not unusual.

Agency directors also find it almost impossible to hire talented individuals from the outside. As one former director said, "It takes a few days short of forever." Robert Powers explains: "If a union position is to be filled—and most are now union—a union member may qualify for the position by experience and training. If a union member qualifies for the position with an A grade, the agency *must* take the union member; if more than one union member is on the A list, the agency *must* take the union member with the most seniority."

Other factors have been at play as well. In the old days, an agency head could bury political appointees in nonessential jobs. With the U.S. Supreme Court–ordered elimination of political hiring in the 1980s, political appointees had to be moved up to policymaking positions, which were exempt from the ban. Often these political appointees are not up to the demanding executive positions in which they find themselves.

Another restriction on hiring is the absolute preference for military veterans. That is, if a veteran is in a group of applicants who received A grades on their exams, the veteran *must* be hired. We believe veterans should be given some preference in hiring, but not absolute preference.

What to do? Here are several recommendations from those experienced in state government management.

75. Prohibit union membership for senior management and supervisory personnel.

76. Reopen the merit compensation pay plan, so that non-union employees know there is a positive career ladder available to them.

77. Provide professional development opportunities for career management employees. With the number of state personnel reduced from 84,000 in 2002 to 64,000 in 2012, those remaining need to benefit from the best management techniques.

78. Conduct a comprehensive assessment of the Illinois Personnel System and agency staffing by an outside human resources firm. The assignment would be to offer recommendations to the governor and the Illinois General Assembly with the following objectives: (1) restoration of morale in the employee corps, which is very low; (2) re-establishment of highly qualified and strongly motivated non-union senior management teams for each state agency, and (3) modernization of the state personnel system, which has out-of-date job descriptions that make it almost impossible to hire the right talent.

79. Eliminate the absolute veterans' preference and replace it with credit for veterans on examinations for state government employment.

80. Change from a broad letter grade system to a numbered grading system, so there is ranking by examination.

Making State Government Operations More Efficient

Tom Johnson chaired the Taxpayers' Action Board (TAB) that was created in 2009 by Governor Quinn; Jim Nowlan was a member of the board, whose members were appointed by the governor. Board members and research staff spent ninety days examining ways in which to reduce the state budget without reducing services. In this section we present options developed by TAB that are worth considering.[10]

The Illinois Department of Transportation employs 3,100 full-time, part-time, and seasonal personnel to maintain the state's highways, at a cost estimated by TAB to be $243 million in 2009. The board suggests comparing competitive private bids against present state costs. An alternative to outsourcing would be "managed competition," in which the public employees would also be asked to bid to provide the highway maintenance services, apportioned by highway district. This would allow for public-private competition and give public employees an opportunity to continue their work if they offer the lowest bids.

81. Conduct "managed competition" for the maintenance of public highways.

Currently, the state requires construction projects to be bid separately, regardless of the project size or task at hand, says TAB. For small and medium construction projects, the result is that vendors must bid again and again for the same types of projects, year after year. This extends the procurement process unnecessarily. The board recommends job-order contracting, which prequalifies vendors so that each vendor's rates and the tasks for which it is qualified are established in advance.

The state essentially develops a master contract with each vendor, and when specific task orders arise, the state can identify the appropriate vendor to fulfill the task. This would move projects ahead more quickly and, TAB estimates, reduce costs by 5 percent compared with the current method because vendors can offer more competitive rates and because the state is better able to predict and plan expenditures and shorten procurement cycles.

82. Enact unit price contracting for state construction projects.

Nobody knows how much real estate Illinois owns, nor how many square feet of building space it owns and leases. According to TAB, the state estimates that it owns and leases about sixty million square feet of space. The board believes that the state should develop a comprehensive real estate strategy and asset inventory under the guidance of a professional services firm, hired in a competitive process, and given responsibility for strategic management as well as portfolio and information management and held accountable for the performance of the portfolio.

The State should consider outsourcing facilities maintenance responsibilities to an appropriately skilled and competitively bid vendor. As part of its review of this opportunity, the state should analyze the present costs of providing maintenance of its facilities.

83. Outsource management of the state's real estate assets to a professional services firm.

84. Outsource facilities maintenance.

Structural Change

If Illinois were today a blank slate, would we draw 102 counties, so that every man could reach his county seat in a day's carriage ride? Would we draw in 1,000 separate police departments? Or would we draw in 6,994 local governments, the largest number of any state in the nation?[11] By separating so many services into independent city, park, recreation, township, and other local governments, we create independent government fiefdoms that are free from healthy competition with one another for limited tax dollars. Virginia manages quite nicely with only 511 local governments.

Why should many of our counties operate nursing homes, which are artifacts of the nineteenth-century county "poor farms," when there are hundreds of private-sector homes? As for our 102 counties, why not consolidate many of the smallest of them, and thus create regional court and criminal justice systems, leaving the shuttered courthouses to local historical societies?

We are at a stage where such thinking, radical to some, we suppose, is required.

When government efficiencies are sought in Illinois, analysts often turn instinctively toward our local governments, knowing that we have more than any state. The obvious notion is that having fewer local governments could generate big savings. As we have found, the savings may or may not result, but there are other reasons for rethinking our local governments.

We have more municipalities (1,296), townships (1,433), school districts (867), and special districts (2,207) than most states. On any given resident's property tax bill, you probably will see between eight and ten different local governments that exact some tax money—city, county, township, schools, community college, fire, park, library, even mosquito abatement and cemetery districts.

In Virginia, in contrast, the cities and counties are responsible for schools and most of the other functions that have separate governments in Illinois. In 2010 Illinois's per capita expenditures by all local governments were higher than the national average; the state spent $5,495 compared with the national average of $5,388. Virginia spent only $4,478 per capita on its local governments.[12]

Illinois probably has more governments than other states for at least a couple of reasons. First, our 1,433 townships are functioning if limited governments; thirty-one states operate without township governments (seventeen counties in southern Illinois also operate without township governments).

Second, a tradition of special, single-purpose local governments may have grown up because of borrowing limitations imposed on local governments by the state constitution that operated from 1870 to 1970. When a city or county ran up against its borrowing limits, local residents simply created a new special unit of government that had its own borrowing powers to create parks, build libraries, buy fire equipment, or build a hospital, among other purposes.

Would we be better off with fewer governments? Yes. For example, in many parts of the state, there are two sets of school districts, one or more school districts for elementary students and another for the overlying high school. Consolidation of the two levels of school districts, creating "dual districts" (as discussed in chapter 3), might ensure a seamless transition from grade to high school.

Townships maintain rural roads and have a welfare function, albeit a very limited one, called "general assistance." Counties could absorb the general assistance function and multi-township road districts could be created.

There is no optimum number of governments. The smaller the unit, the greater the role for local democracy in overseeing the government. Can there be, however, so much local government that citizens are unable to oversee it all? Fewer and larger governments also provide economies of scale.

The political scientist Christopher Berry finds that overlapping governments such as those in Illinois appear to tax and spend more in total that general-purpose governments that offer the same services. Berry finds that increases in jurisdictional overlap lead to increases in the public budget.[13] He cites the lack of competition for resources within insulated special district governments. In addition, the single-purpose special districts have their own interest groups to serve by funding the objectives of these groups, without much fear of retribution at the polls.

Other states that have also looked at the issue tend to recommend that functions like those of special districts and townships be melded into county governments.

Professor Ann Lousin of the John Marshall Law School is an expert on Illinois government. Lousin proposes a simple plan for dramatic reduction in local governments: within five years, every local government other than school districts that lies 95 percent within a municipality be consolidated into that municipality, and every local government that lies 95 percent within a county be consolidated into that county. That would eliminate most special districts and all townships.[14]

In 2013 DuPage County board chair Dan Cronin led successful efforts in the legislature to authorize his board, alone among the state's counties, to dissolve by ordinance outdated or defunct county-appointed agencies. Voters have an opportunity to block such eliminations through back-door referendums. The legislation could affect appointed governmental agencies that provide public services such as sanitation, mosquito abatement, fire protection (without full-time employees), and street lighting.

Elimination or consolidation of some of our many local governments will not address our state and local budget woes in any significant way. That shouldn't reduce efforts by reformers who seek elimination or consolidation where doing so would make government less expensive and more rational, efficient, and easy to follow.

85. The General Assembly should authorize county boards throughout Illinois to dissolve or consolidate local governments whose members are appointed by the county board, when they can make a case that taxpayer savings would result and that necessary services would not suffer.

86. Eliminate the township form of government by transferring the limited welfare function of townships to county governments and by creating multi-township road districts in place of the township road function.

87. The General Assembly should enact a plan to integrate special districts and townships into municipalities and counties within five years.

Public Policy

In 1970 Illinois prisons held 7,300 inmates. As of 2013, there were 49,000 prisoners in a system with a rated capacity of 32,782.[15] It costs the state about $21,500 per year to maintain each inmate. In the 1970s Illinois spent about 2 percent of its general funds on corrections; by 2013 that figure had doubled to 4 percent, $1.3 billion.

Forty-four percent of all inmates are in prison for drugs or property-related crimes. About half of all Illinois prison inmates return to prison within three years of their release.[16] Twenty-five percent are in prison because of technical violations of their parole, for example, missing a scheduled meeting with a parole officer.

Pat Quinn's 2009 Taxpayers' Action Board (TAB) recommended that prison rolls be reduced over time by 15,000, from 49,000 to 34,000, with the nonviolent offenders instead placed on parole or probation, at a savings of approximately $375 million per year.[17]

So, the state could save money if more nonviolent, low-level criminals were diverted from prison to local drug treatment programs and home confinement. One promising state program is Adult Redeploy Illinois. The state provides funding to county justice systems that pledge to divert at least 25 percent of their adult clients from prison to drug and alcohol treatment programs and probation services. In 2011–12 the ten sites of Adult Redeploy Illinois have diverted 838 nonviolent offenders, or the equivalent of two cellblocks of a prison.[18] Sites spent an average of $2,233 per participant, about one-tenth the cost of housing an inmate in the state prison system. Illinois Redeploy is a similar program that diverts juvenile justice offenders from the state's youth centers.

One of the realities of incarceration policy in Illinois is the transferring of costs from local governments to the state by sending local miscreants to the state prisons and saying, "He's your problem (and cost) now." With state financial assistance available to local justice systems to keep nonviolent lawbreakers in local programs, many local governments should make more effort than they do. There need to be stronger partnerships between state and local social service and justice programs to keep more persons out of expensive state prisons.

Thus far a financial carrot has been used to seek voluntary efforts at the county level to divert more lawbreakers from state prisons. Maybe it is time for the state to use a stick on counties that abuse the use of overcrowded state prison space. This could be done by charging a housing fee to counties that send higher-than-typical percentages of their violators to the state correctional system.

88. Expand Adult Redeploy Illinois (adults) and Illinois Redeploy (juveniles) so that all counties can participate. (See sidebar nearby.)

89. Establish a range of typical state incarceration rates for county justice systems and charge housing fees for each inmate above that range sent to the state correctional system.

The TAB also proposed that the Illinois Department of Corrections work to identify the undocumented immigrants in the prison system and seek to have them deported.[19] A study by IDOC suggests there could be as many as 1,700 undocumented immigrants in Illinois correctional centers; removing them via deportation would represent a savings of about $51 million annually. Taxpayers should not be responsible for supporting these persons. To prevent the return of these offenders, Illinois should enact measures that impose the strongest possible sanctions against deportees who return to the state.

90. Deport undocumented immigrants in the Illinois Department of Corrections.

In terms of prison management, TAB recommended that the Department of Corrections shift from a standard eight-hour, five-day work week to a twelve-hour, four-day work schedule. The department states that it requires fewer employees to operate a facility with twelve-hour shifts and that such a change could result in savings of $31 million a year.[20]

91. Shift prison guards from a regular work week to a twelve-hour, four-day work week.

Juvenile Justice Reform: Reducing Inmate Numbers

Ogle County State's Attorney (now circuit judge) John B. "Ben" Roe made a name for himself by keeping people out of prison, rather than for "throwing the book at them." Roe and a team of professionals funded in part by the MacArthur Foundation of Chicago diverted hundreds of troubled juveniles from the court system. And they say it's paying off in reduced crime and lower numbers in the system of courts, jails, and juvenile prisons. The program continues.

The idealistic thirty-eight-year-old Roe is a former staffer at a program for troubled youth in Ogle County, south of Rockford. He followed that job with a stint as an assistant prosecuting attorney whose responsibilities included juvenile cases. The first time he saw a youth was in court—and his job was to put the youngster away. It made no sense to Roe. "Studies show," says Roe, "that 75 percent of youngsters who have spent time in a juvenile detention facility will end up back in prison later in life."

Roe and veteran probation officer Greg Martin as well as others on a county juvenile justice council started with the schools to identify and work with youngsters at risk of getting into trouble.

When a youngster does commit vandalism, drug offenses, or some other unlawful act, the council swings into further action. The simple and easy path would be to charge the youngster with a felony (damage costing more than $300 constitutes a felony). Ogle County avoids the easy path.

Instead, every juvenile case reported by police is assessed promptly by mental health and community specialists. And if, for example, diversion from the court system is seen as the best course in a vandalism case, the ideal first step in the diversion process is victim-offender counseling. "There is an unbelievable dynamic here," says Roe, "as the youngster must confront face-to-face the victim of his or her damaging actions."

"You know how much this cost me?" asks the victim of the youngster. "Why me?" The youngster is almost always without an answer.

After the session, a mediator works out a proposal, which might entail cleaning up the damage, doing public service work, or making monetary restitution.

If a youngster completes the agreed-on tasks in the allotted time, the case is closed, and when the offender reaches age seventeen the information about the offense is automatically expunged from court records. (Few realize that even before a case reaches court, the information from the police report about the arrest and fingerprinting becomes part of a court record and can pop up years later when a person seeks a job, unless expunged.)

Other tools available to the juvenile justice council include substance abuse treatment, "community impact panels," in which a range of community leaders meet with offenders, and cognitive behavior groups, in which a therapist reviews with the offender the steps he or she went through prior to committing the offense.

In cases that are not diverted from the court system, a prompt assessment of the offender is still conducted; the therapist is present at the arraignment in court. Through a memorandum of understanding, the prosecutor's office agrees not to use information elicited in the assessment. And indeed, public defenders often learn valuable information about their client that they would not otherwise have. Sometimes the assessment results in dismissal of the case, directing it instead to the diversion process.

At other times, court supervision is recommended rather than probation; supervision keeps the youngster from becoming a ward of the court and labeled a delinquent.

Of five hundred police contacts with minors in Ogle County since 2008, 70 percent have been diverted away from court and only 5 percent of those youths have been rearrested. Before then, much higher percentages of cases went to the court system and rearrests were higher as well, says Roe, although no one kept such data before 2008.

Roe notes that diversion costs less than $400 per youngster, whereas the figure is more than $1,200 for those going through the court system.

"We call is being smart, not soft, on crime," Roe says.

The MacArthur Foundation provides funding, for example, for training of probation officers in functional family therapy. A probation officer can take the intensive training and go into a home and work with the whole family, which is often where a big part of the problem lies.

But can a program that appears to work in a rural county of fifty-five thousand people with a strong sense of community be replicated on the mean streets of an urban setting? Roe thinks so. He points to New York City, where, he believes, similar concepts have been applied effectively.

Decades ago, when Jim Nowlan was a young man in a rural county, he recalled the phrase spoken about a juvenile delinquent: "We can't handle him here, so let's send him up to St. Charles" (then as now a youth "reformatory" or center). We still do that too often, at a cost of $86,000 per year for each of the 900 young people in the state's youth centers.

Seventy percent of the youth are in the statewide system for non-violent crimes or for technical violations of their parole. Better to develop less expensive programs at home for the nonviolent among the youthful offenders.

Legislative Process

We believe the Illinois General Assembly can become a more effective contributor to policymaking in Illinois than it has been. We feel that the legislature has become fragmented and has lost focus on the fundamental issues that face the state. For example, the House had thirty-eight committees and the Senate twenty-six as of 2013. In addition, there are short-term committees formed to study both narrow and major issues. As a result, we sense that the legislature is not doing as good a job as it could in developing legislators who are respected experts on critical topics such as Medicaid, human services, transportation, and the budget. This is not to take anything away from the very bright, highly knowledgeable lawmakers who at present are looked to for their experience with these and other important topics. We simply feel that they could become even more steeped in their respective areas of expertise with additional organizational support.

Prior to the 1980s the legislature benefited from the expertise developed by members who served on several permanent joint legislative study commissions that welcomed expert members of the public. They included the commissions on revenue laws, pension laws, public aid, education, election laws, and transportation as well as the powerful Budgetary Commission. These bodies met throughout the year, with members often serving a number of years. Over time, the chairs as well as other members of these commissions became respected experts in their respective subject matter, and they served as good overseers of state agencies responsible for their areas of interest. The public members of each commission were often academic experts in their fields. Reports were prepared for each commission to consider.

The General Assembly today has impressive staffing that could support the work of such permanent study commissions. We feel that they would add extra depth to the capacity of the legislature to analyze important problems and offer thoughtful policy solutions.

92. Reestablish in the Illinois General Assembly's permanent joint legislative and public member study commissions on the fundamental issues facing Illinois.

Collective bargaining agreements with state employees' unions are negotiated by the governor and his staff. There are situations in which the governor has an incentive to please the unions during bargaining, in order to receive their political support during subsequent elections. This may have happened during the 2010 bargaining cycle, which occurred the summer prior to the November election. Nevertheless, subsequent state legislatures are required to fulfill the contractual obligations entered into by the executive branch.

In Connecticut, by comparison, the legislature has authority to approve or reject any collective bargaining agreements reached between the governor and state unions. Under the terms of the Connecticut Public Labor Relations Act, any collective bargaining agreement shall be filed with that state's House and Senate within ten days after such an agreement is reached: "The General Assembly may approve any such agreement as a whole by a majority vote in each house or may reject any such agreement by a majority vote in either house. The General Assembly may reject any such (arbitration) award as a whole by a two-thirds vote of either house if it determines there are insufficient funds for full implementation of the award. If rejected, the matter shall be returned to the parties for further bargaining."[21] Such a provision in Illinois law would tend to protect against any sweetheart contracts that would bind subsequent legislatures.

93. Provide in law that the Illinois General Assembly must approve or reject collective bargaining agreements reached between the executive branch and state employees' unions.

The varied recommendations presented in this chapter represent starting points for possible improvements in the operations, structure, policies, and processes of our state and local governments. We hope that they will stimulate thinking about ways in which to make positive change.

CHAPTER 8

Corruption in Illinois

An Enduring Tradition

Corruption has been an enduring habit in Illinois and Chicago governments throughout the state's history. And habits are hard to break.

In this chapter we discuss the realities and perceptions of this corruption and the costs the perceptions impose on Illinois.[1] We also offer observations about and options for transforming the culture of corruption that we believe exists in the state. We begin by noting that corruption is anything but a recent phenomenon in Illinois

Corruption through Illinois History

Ninian Edwards served as both the territorial governor of Illinois (1809–1818) and the third elected governor of the state (1826–30). Early in our statehood, he issued prescient warning about the corrupting role of money in elections by decrying what he called the "common practice" of the time of "treating" prospective voters with whisky to win their votes.[2] Those who do so, declared Edwards, "establish a school of vice and depravity in our country tending to contaminate not only the present but succeeding generations. . . The precedent, once established, will become less and less objectionable by becoming more familiar to you; it will finally become fashionable, and ultimately necessary to success. . . . All distinctions will then be confined to the rich, for they alone will be able to meet the expenses of an election."[3]

The history of vote fraud in Chicago elections goes back to at least 1884. In *Grafters and Goo Goos* (2004), James L. Merriner takes a romp through corruption in the Chicago area from 1883 to 2003 and of efforts to combat it. He notes, for example, that reformers were highly suspicious of the mayoral victory in 1884 of Carter Harrison Sr.[4] So the Union League Club of Chicago hired detectives to investigate a typical precinct. The sleuths found that George Washington, Thomas Jefferson, John Hancock, and other notables had registered and voted. (Merriner notes that parallel ruses were discovered in a 1969 investigation of vote fraud in Chicago.) Of 1,112 votes cast in the precinct, 907 were fraudulent. Of 171 precincts ultimately examined, only 7 seemed to be without irregularities.

By the 1890s, declares Robert J. Schoenberg, "Chicago routinized corruption as never before—politicians, police, prosecutors, defense bar, judiciary, citizenry and lawbreakers became so bound by ties of graft, bribery and intimidation that honesty appeared eccentric."[5] During this decade, streetcar magnate Charles T. Yerkes paid bribes of up to $50,000 each to Chicago aldermen in return for particularly favorable franchises. Yerkes simply bought most of the 68 members of the city council. He set market prices for council favors: $100 for a saloon license and $500 to restore a license that had been revoked for cause.[6] The $200-per-year job of alderman became worth $25,000, often more, to the boodling lawmakers (a boodler is one who participates in graft).

Yerkes also tried, with some success, to buy the state legislature. The bribery was so blatant that a reporter for the *Chicago Evening Journal* was inadvertently offered money for his vote. Sitting in the seat of a member of the House before the day's session got under way, the journalist was mistaken for that member by a near-sighted old state senator. "The lawmaker sat down beside me," recalled the reporter, "and opened with the explicit statement he would pay $2,500 for my vote on the traction bill. He quickly discovered his mistake, and there was much scurrying in the ranks of the grafters."[7]

In 1909, supporters of Congressman William J. Lorimer created a national sensation when they apparently paid $100,000 in bribes to as many as forty state lawmakers in Springfield to elect Lorimer to the United States Senate.[8] Bribes of up to $2,500 per bribed lawmaker were split between pre-vote payments and a post-session "jackpot" of payments from the major interest groups to lawmakers who had voted in their interests. (At the time, a new Model T Ford cost $850.) See figure 9, an editorial cartoon from a 1910 edition of the Des Moines Register, which depicts the bemusement of observers of corruption in Illinois. In 1912 Lorimer was expelled from the United States Senate on the ground that he would not have been elected absent the brib-

FIGURE 9. "What's the Matter with Illinois?" by J. N. "Ding" Darling

Source: *Des Moines Register*, August 10, 1910. University of Iowa Libraries: Iowa Digital Library.

ery. The scandal generated renewed interest in passage of the Seventeenth Amendment to the U.S. Constitution, adopted in 1913, which provides for popular election of senators.

By the time Al Capone came to town a few years later, one alderman declared, "Chicago is unique. It is the only completely corrupt city in America."[9] In such an environment and with much of the citizenry thirsty for the beer and spirits prohibited by the Eighteenth Amendment to the U.S. Constitution, "a Capone became not just logical but inevitable."[10] Capone and his gangs gained power through the corruption already in place, through willing accomplices in government, and through the citizenry. During the reigns of mayor William Hale (Big Bill) Thompson and of the supportive Capone, Police Chief Charles Fitzmorris admitted that about half of his force of six thousand was involved in bootlegging—not only soliciting and receiving bribes but actively pushing alcohol.[11] Merriner writes, "The Bureau of Internal Revenue estimated the 1927 income of Capone's gang at $100 million, of which $10 million was Capone's profit. Thirty million dollars was budgeted for graft to buy politicians and the police."[12]

As Kenneth Alsop observes, writing of Chicago, "[a]fter the start of Prohibition, who was the crook? Millions of people who regarded themselves as upright, law-respecting . . . began . . . to cheat and lie, and entered into routine conspiracy with the underworld."[13] As Capone once put it: "Nobody's on the legit. . . . Your brother or your father gets in a jam. What do you do? Do you sit back and let him go over the road, without trying to help him? You'd be a yellow dog if you did. Nobody's legit when it comes down to cases."[14]

Corruption was so pervasive in the Capone era that contemporary observers said even honest politicians "had to make compromises with evil, in their judgment, in order to create a greater good."[15] The system, as it had developed, made them do it.

In 1956, Illinois Auditor of Public Accounts Orville Hodge pleaded guilty to stealing at least $1.5 million from state coffers.[16] At that time, the auditor of public accounts was responsible for doing both the pre-audit and the post-audit of Illinois spending. So, for several years, Hodge was able to issue warrants to persons who had formerly done business with the state and have the warrants secretly cashed.

Not even the state's high court was immune from at least charges of ethical lapses. In 1969, Illinois Supreme Court chief justice Roy Solfisburg and former chief justice Raymond Klingbiel resigned, under great pressure, from the high court because of the appearance of improprieties.[17] The two justices had received stock in a new bank issued by Theodore Isaacs at a time circuit court charges against Isaacs for defrauding the state were being dismissed by the state Supreme Court in a decision written by Klingbiel.

In 1970, when Illinois Secretary of State Paul Powell died, he left behind $800,000 in large bills stuffed in shoeboxes and found in his Springfield hotel room.[18]

The most distressing examples of public corruption were brought to light in the late 1980s and early 1990s as a result of Operations Greylord and Gambat, U.S. Department of Justice investigations into the court system of Cook County.[19] Nearly one hundred court officials and lawyers, including eighteen judges, were convicted of systematic bribery as a result of Operation Greylord. Operation Gambat used a corrupt lawyer turned informant to reveal that associates of the Chicago Mob were paying off judges to dismiss cases against even murderers and hitmen. Operation Gambat resulted in convictions of twenty-four corrupt judges, lawyers, and police officers, including the presiding judge of the Chancery Court, the assistant majority leader of the Illinois State Senate, and a judge convicted of fixing murder cases, the only such judge in the United States.

Since 1980 a total of thirty Chicago aldermen have been convicted of federal crimes such as bribery, extortion, embezzlement, conspiracy, mail fraud, and tax evasion.[20]

The Illinois convictions included a first in 2003 when the George Ryan Campaign Committee, rather than a person, was convicted of racketeering. In 2006 Ryan himself was convicted on all twenty-four counts with which he was charged, including racketeering, mail fraud, filing false tax returns, and lying to investigators. Indeed, four of the past seven governors (Otto Kerner, Dan Walker, George Ryan, and Rod Blagojevich) have been found guilty of wrongdoing by federal courts.

Rod Blagojevich became governor in 2003 on a reform platform, proclaiming that there would be "no more business as usual" in Illinois government. In 2006, however, a top fundraiser and advisor to Blagojevich named Antoine (Tony) Rezko was indicted on twenty-four counts of corruption in what U.S. Attorney Patrick Fitzgerald called "a pay-to-play scheme on steroids."[21] Prosecutors accused Rezko of "trying to collect nearly $6 million in kickbacks from government deals and trying to shake down a Hollywood producer for $1.5 million in campaign contributions to Blagojevich."[22] Blagojevich himself was convicted on June 27, 2011, of seventeen criminal counts, including wire fraud, attempted extortion, bribery, and conspiracy, on top of an earlier conviction for lying to the FBI.[23]

In 2006 the *Chicago Tribune* ran an editorial titled "Corruption on Parade," which declared, "But as you plow through the daily digest of indictments, not-guilty pleas, convictions, the occasional acquittal, sentencings and look-whose-heading-off-to-prison stories, it's possible to lose the big picture. This is a unique time in Illinois. . . . Illinois produces enough guilty pleas for these kinds of crimes to establish that this state's problem is close to unique."[24]

Realities and Perceptions of Corruption in Illinois

By some measures Illinois is among the most corrupt states in the nation. According to an analysis of U.S. Department of Justice reports of convictions for public corruption from 1976 to 2010, 1,828 persons in Illinois have been found guilty during this time frame, more than in any states but New York and California.[25] On a per capita basis, Illinois ranked third among the large states in public corruption convictions. The United States District Court for the Northern District of Illinois (metropolitan Chicago) tallied more convictions for public corruption over a thirty-five-year period than did any district court in the nation.[26]

And that represents only the illegal corruption. Illinois officials have become masters of milking our governments and taxpayers through legal corruption. We are deeply disturbed, for example, by the 2011 *Chicago Tribune* investigation that found that Chicago alderman Edward Burke doubled the annual pension of his buddy, former state representative Bob Molaro, to $120,000.[27] Burke had Molaro work for just one month at $12,000, which created an annualized salary rate that qualified him for the doubling of his legislative pension. What did Molaro do to earn the $12,000? He wrote a paper about the sorry state of our public pension systems, basically laughing at the taxpayers who will pay the extra pension benefits for Molaro! For too many public officials in Illinois, doing well in public office comes before doing good for the public.

By other measures, however, Illinois is in the middle of the pack when it comes to corruption. Professor Richard Winters at Dartmouth College points out that if the numbers of elected officials per state are considered (Illinois has more than forty thousand, far more than most states, because we have more units of local government than any state), then Illinois is really about average in terms of convictions for public corruption per thousand elected state and local officials.[28]

Yet reality may lie in the eye of the beholder, and when it comes to perception, Illinois consistently ranks among the most corrupt states in the nation. For example, in a 2012 poll that we conducted, one-third of those surveyed identified Illinois, unsolicited, as such, following only New York and California. And a full 45 percent of the respondents over age thirty-five named Illinois as one of the most corrupt states.[29] Other Midwestern states were rarely mentioned as among the most corrupt, which means that Illinois sticks out like a sore thumb in the heartland region.

Journalists believe Illinois to be one of the most corrupt states as well. In 2000, Richard Boylan and Cheryl Long surveyed journalists nationwide, who ranked Illinois third highest in corruption among the forty-five states with usable numbers of responses.[30]

Widely held perceptions such as these are also bad for business in Illinois. In the national survey cited above, 60 percent of the respondents said knowing about corruption in a state would have a negative or strongly negative effect on their decisions to locate in such a state.[31]

Possibly more important is a 2011 survey we took of seventy economic development professionals in Illinois (the people who work to attract business to a community). Three in four surveyed said corruption in Illinois had a negative impact on their business recruiting.[32] Among the forty-nine written responses to this question, two provide particular insight. One says, "Unfortunately and especially in manufacturing and international circles, there is an understanding that corruption in Illinois that once occurred at an individual level has moved to systemic corruption." The other states, "As part of an economic development marketing group that spans Illinois and Iowa, I keep hearing that Iowa makes sense as a business location if you just want to fill out an application and have a transparent process. Illinois works better if you have political clout and are willing to use it. I think that is a travesty and that is what Illinois is becoming known for—pay to play."

What has come to be called "the Chicago Way" or "the Illinois Way" of public corruption has likely undermined the voters' sense of political efficacy.[33] Why apply for a city or state job if you think that only friends of political insiders will be hired? Why report corrupt officials if you think they won't be punished and that the system may turn the powers of government on you instead? Voters may sometimes laugh at the antics of corrupt public officials, but in the end they feel powerless, lose their faith in government, and vote less often because they believe that the fix is in. Lilliard Richardson found in his study of the 2008 national elections that "convictions (for public corruption) per capita are strongly associated with lower political activity across the board."[34]

And there are tangible costs to corruption. Political scientist Dick Simpson estimates that it costs Illinois and its governments $500 million each year. "Governor Blagojevich's well-publicized corruption antics" he writes, "led to a lowering of the state's bond rating, which cost the state more than $20 million during a recent bond issue. Corruption also takes time and resources away from police and prosecutors. Blagojevich's first trial costs tens of millions of dollars to investigate and prosecute."[35]

Observations

Why is there so much corruption, or at least the strong perception of corruption, in Illinois?

In the 1970s the late student of American federalism Daniel Elazar contended that the United States was divided into three historical political subcultures: the moralistic, the traditionalistic, and the individualistic. In brief, the moralistic culture tends to see government as a positive force and believe that politicians are not expected to profit from political activity. Minnesota, Wisconsin, and Michigan are dominated, in Elazar's construct, by this set of cultural attitudes.[36]

The traditionalistic culture tends to be operated by an elite that sees government as a means for maintaining the existing social order, and corruption by government officials is tolerated as a way of maintaining that order. This culture dominates in the Deep South. The individualistic culture sees government as a necessary evil that should be limited so as not to affect the individual's private business activities. Corrupt politics is accepted as a fact and is tolerated.

Illinois is dominated overall by the individualistic culture, according to Elazar, though he notes that southern Illinois is influenced heavily by the traditionalistic culture. Yet because two of the three political subcultures tolerate corruption, this framework, if there is anything to it, provides limited help in separating Illinois from other states.

We also subscribe to the additional theory that immigrants such as the Irish, Italians, and Poles found it difficult to enter legitimate businesses in Chicago that were dominated by the white Anglo-Saxon Protestants who preceded them. Thus, they used their growing numbers to win at the business of politics, where many of them developed the tradition of providing government jobs in return for political support and of doing well as much as doing good.

Another reason why corruption exists some places but not others (at least, not as much), according to Michael Josephson, is that "corruption flourishes because it is allowed. Whatever you allow, you encourage."[37] In this regard, for example, the Illinois General Assembly lacks a "revolving door" prohibition, that is, one that would bar legislators from lobbying members of the General Assembly for at least one year after they leave the legislature. As a result, in 2012 several members of the Assembly resigned in the middle of their terms to take lobbying positions with interest groups with whom they had close legislative ties. Nobody in the political world of the General Assembly seemed to think much about it.

94. Enact a revolving-door prohibition for Illinois state legislators, barring them from lobbying members of the General Assembly for at least one year after they leave the legislature.

We also think that over the course of the past century our culture has developed an underlying sense that, for some of us, taking advantage of government is the thing to do, since everyone else does it.

For example, for several years Jim Nowlan conducted an exercise with his students at the University of Illinois at the beginning of his courses in American politics.[38] Most of the students were seniors, many headed for law school. Semester after semester, two-thirds of the students would opt for using bribery to get a brother out of a particularly burdensome DUI charge. The students rationalized their decisions with such observations as, "Everyone else does it" and "We'd be played the fools for not doing so for our brother."

Moreover, we simply don't think about the ethics of our actions. Rare is the person who enters politics planning to be corrupt. Some cynics would say that in Chicago that should read "planning to be caught." Why are so many in our state measured for striped suits when that wasn't our objective? When Jim Nowlan entered the Illinois legislature as a young man in the late 1960s, he had not previously thought about the fact that private gain could be made at public expense (our definition of corruption). He could easily have gone along with the way some people played the game and accepted "contributions" at about the same time action was taken on certain bills.

Fortunately, in his freshman year the late George O'Brien (a freshman legislator like Nowlan, and later a congressman) sent copies of the play *A Man for All Seasons* to his fellow freshmen. The play is about Thomas More, who rejected King Henry VIII's demand for a divorce. More stood on principle and paid the ultimate price with his head. Though far removed from the Illinois General Assembly, the play struck Nowlan like a thunderbolt. There are indeed matters of principle at play in politics, and one must be aware when they arise. And sometimes it may be difficult to stand up to a corrupt system. Ninety-seven Cook County court officials were convicted of bribery and related charges in the 1980s in Operation Greylord. Some may have lacked the fortitude to challenge the system in which they became caught up.

Maybe some cannot resist the temptation of financial gain based on inside knowledge or actions, and figure they won't be caught. In this day and age, it is best to assume that everything will be found out!

Several years ago, a young friend of Nowlan's moved back after college to his hometown, where he ran for mayor as a reformer against the ossified "old guard." Walking door to door, this friend won the full-time job of mayor. A few weeks later, he was at a national mayors' conference in Washington, DC, hob-nobbing with Willie Brown of San Francisco and Rudy Giuliani of New York City.

In college this big farm boy had played football in a Big Ten program, and now he proudly wore a Rose Bowl ring, a good conversation starter when he was with Willie and Rudy. Yet the friend realized that he looked shabby without a suit. So he quickly bought a suit in Washington, using his city's credit card, the only one he had, planning to pay the city back.

Later the purchase became a *cause célèbre* in his small city. And it tarnished his otherwise fine reputation. We worry about the good guys who, like the young ex-mayor, have not thought about the fish bowl they are jumping into.

For the good guys who are newcomers to politics, we present our "Guide to Ethical Decision-making in the Twenty-First Century":

- Don't be careless. Even the slightest inadvertent indiscretion will get you. People do care—and do find out. It doesn't matter what *you* think about what you did. If others think it's indiscreet, it is. If it looks bad, it is.
- Is there any dimension of any decision you make that could be seen by others as personal gain at public expense? Or, as former Illinois auditor general Robert Cronson put it, "How would this sound to a grand jury?"
- Never justify a decision on the basis that "this is the way it has always been done." Times change. In the 1950s a federal jury acquitted Illinois governor William Stratton on charges of paying for, among other things, evening attire for his wife from campaign funds and not reporting the expenditures as income. Today, how would the jury find him on similar charges? We would bet "guilty."
- Identify a friend or acquaintance whom you respect for his or her integrity. (Ours would be Mike Lawrence, former head of the Paul Simon Public Policy Institute.) Have him serve as your second opinion; how would he view a pending decision?
- If you have questions about a decision, assume it's the wrong thing to do.

Ethics and Cultural Change

Yale political scientist Susan Rose-Ackerman declares that "corruption in all its myriad forms arises at the intersection of culture, the market, and the state. Its prevalence forces us to confront the tangled connections between private wealth and public power and between cultural practice and the creation of a competent and impartial government."[39] As for reform, she notes that simple transparency is necessary as well as external oversight of government activity by investigative journalists.

We think Illinois suffers from a culture of corruption, as exhibited earlier by the university students who opted for bribery to help a hypothetical brother avoid a criminal charge. Charles Snyder is a retired executive at John Deere in Moline, Illinois, who was involved with efforts at cultural change at his company during the difficult early 1980s. He identifies the following factors as important:

- Leadership: authoritative, visionary, charismatic;
- Creation of a group identity;
- Defining a compelling need to change;
- Communicating the need for change; and
- Obtaining buy-in to change: shared sacrifice and not just asking "What's in it for me?"[40]

Susan Heathfield says executive support and training are critical: "Executives in the organization must support the cultural change," she writes," "and in ways beyond verbal support. They must show behavioral support by changing their own behaviors."[41] Heathfield adds that since cultural change depends on behavioral change, training can be very useful in both communicating expectations and teaching new behaviors.

Cultural attitudes and behavior can change. Political scientist Robert Rich calls this process "public learning."[42] Think of society's attitudes toward drinking and driving. When the authors were young, little thought was given to the issue. As a result of major campaigns by such groups as Mothers Against Drunk Driving and changes in law, public behavior has changed significantly, and the number of deaths caused by drunk drivers is down because of it. Similarly, when we were young, smoking was popular and "cool." Today it is definitely not, and our collective lifespan has been increased.

Rich identifies several factors that have been shown to be important in achieving public learning. These include convincing evidence that an activity such as smoking is bad for people and society as well as continuing support from the media. In addition, change based on public learning needs a highly visible champion. For example, former U.S. surgeon general C. Everett Koop championed cessation of smoking and Mothers Against Drunk Driving continue their efforts to reduce driving under the influence of alcohol.

Positive change can be accomplished. According to Dick Simpson, a political scientist at the University of Illinois at Chicago, major cities such as

Hong Kong and Sydney, Australia, have gone from corrupt to clean.[43] And Chicago itself has a historical case in which a corrupt majority of the city council was driven from office. At the turn of the twentieth century, the Municipal Voters' League and its dynamic leader George E. Cole raised money, recruited candidates, ran campaigns, and elected honest men to the Chicago City Council.[44] According to Charles Merriam, who was then both a city councilman and a professor at the University of Chicago, the Voters' League "gave the city the best legislative body in the country for 20 years."[45] But by the 1920s, the fervor of the league's volunteer efforts had waned, and corrupt politics returned.

In their book *Nudge* (2008), University of Chicago business professors Richard Thaler and Cass Sunstein posit that behavior can be changed by seemingly small psychological adjustments that they call "change architecture."[46] A change architect might, for example, rearrange the presentation and placement of foods in a student cafeteria to increase or decrease the selection of certain foods. Another example: after years of frustration and lack of success, the State of Texas reduced littering on its highways by 72 percent in six years by developing the "Don't Mess with Texas" slogan and advertising program. The slogan focused on youth between eighteen and twenty-four who were doing most of the littering with "a tough-talking slogan that would also address the unique spirit of Texas pride." Dallas Cowboy stars and Willie Nelson were among those featured in the advertising campaign.

The illustration above is from the chapter called "Following the Herd," which, boiled down to its essence, holds that people have a tendency to do what they think other people are doing.[47] And thus, Thaler and Sunstein write, "[a] few influential people, offering strong signals about appropriate behavior, can have a similar effect (of changing behavior)."

In addition to promoting cultural change, what can we do about corruption through changes in public policy? Illinois already has fairly stringent state ethics laws. In her book *The Shadowlands of Conduct: Ethics and State Politics*, Beth Rosenson rates Illinois at 8.5 on a scale in which 10.5 is the maximum. She notes that Illinois has a basic ethics code, limits on honoraria and gifts, and a requirement of personal financial disclosure.[48] This rating places Illinois higher on the scale than most states. The only criterion of Rosenson's that Illinois lacks is a limit on lobbying employment for former state legislators (see Suggestion 94, above). The Illinois ethics law was first promulgated in 1967 and has been amended in 1972, 1995, 2003, and 2009.

The 2003 Illinois Ethics Act, as amended in 2009, provided for inspectors general, executive and legislative ethics commissions, annual ethics training for state employees, whistleblower protections, and other changes. Unfortunately, according to Illinois Legislative Inspector General Thomas J. Homer, the 2003 legislation did not address the significant shortcomings of the 1967 Ethics Act, which established a code of conduct and ethical principles for legislators and required the disclosure of economic interests but failed to provide sanctions for violations.[49] In a 2011 letter to members of the General Assembly, Homer noted that since 1972, fifteen state legislators and four governors had been convicted of crimes, but when the Code of Conduct was adopted in 1967, the legislature not only provided no penalties but expressly stated that the ethical principles "are intended only as guides [for conduct], and not as rules meant to be enforced by disciplinary action." Homer went on to recommend that "violations of the Code of Conduct should be modernized and be made punishable by fines, public reporting and censure. These rules should not be merely aspirational goals."

> 95. Make violations of the Illinois General Assembly's Code of Conduct punishable by fines, public reporting, and censure.

In a 2012 poll of 1,200 Illinois residents, three of four respondents disagreed (most of them strongly) with the statement "Nothing can be done about corruption in our state."[50] So public support for anti-corruption efforts should be strong.

There are at least two approaches that can be taken to dampen public corruption: legislation that changes the environment in which politics is conducted, and public awareness campaigns that increase sensitivity to the ethical and moral consequences of decision making in government.

In the legislation category, we champion public financing of campaigns, which could increase competition in elections and reduce, among some candidates, reliance on large contributions. Public financing of some elections exists in about half the states. The typical approach is that a candidate for office who draws a threshold number of small contributions, in order to show the candidate's credibility, receives matching funds for all of his or her small contributions or receives a set amount of money and agrees not to raise any more.

In addition, we strongly advocate an amendment to the Illinois Constitution that would replace partisan gerrymandering of state legislative districts with an independent commission, as is the case in Arizona and California. The commission would ideally draw district lines without regard to incumbency and with regard for somewhat natural communities of interest where that might be possible.

The current process in Illinois almost guarantees that leaders of one of the two major parties will draw state legislative and congressional district boundaries. With the technique of packing partisans of the respective parties into districts, incumbents have been protected and electoral competition has been stifled.

96. Enact public financing of campaigns in Illinois, perhaps beginning with campaigns for judicial offices as a way of introducing the policy.

97. Enact by citizens' initiative an amendment to the Legislative Article of the Illinois Constitution to create an independent commission to draw state legislative district boundaries without regard to incumbency.

98. As for public awareness campaigns, we recommend the following:

- Governors should take responsibility for providing continuing and visible leadership in setting the highest standards of ethical conduct and for continually exhorting citizens to conduct that will transform "the Illinois Way" into a model for integrity in government and politics.
- Mandate that of the two years of social science courses required in Illinois high schools, at least one semester be devoted to American government and civics.
- Provide lesson plans for Illinois social science teachers that address ethics in personal life and ethics in government.
- Provide workshops on ethics in government for newly elected state legislators, as well as those in city, county, school board, and other local governments.

Illinois has a reputation for corruption in government. Actual corruption and the reputation for corruption both impose their costs on our society. We need to mount major campaigns of corruption abatement in Illinois to show the world that we are committed to high ethical standards. We need to begin now. After all, habits are hard to break.

In our small book about the state of Illinois we have attempted to touch on the bigger challenges facing Illinois and to offer suggestions, some major and some more modest, for addressing these challenges. We hope this is but the beginning of a substantive discussion of the strengths and weaknesses of the suggestions in these pages and of your prescriptions for what might be done to right the ship of state, which we think has been listing badly. Let the constructive conversations begin.

Notes

Introduction. The Future of Illinois

1. "Americans Love Hawaii, Dislike California," Public Policy Polling, Raleigh, NC, from a press release, February 21, 2012.

2. Richard C. Longworth, *Caught in the Middle: America's Heartland in the Age of Globalism* (New York: Bloomsbury, 2008).

3. Illinois Integrity Initiative Survey, Institute of Government and Public Affairs, University of Illinois, Urbana, December 2011. The survey was taken for the initiative by Kelton Research, New York, NY, and Culver City, CA.

4. 2012 Illinois Policy Survey, Center for Governmental Studies, Northern Illinois University, DeKalb. The Institute of Government and Public Affairs at the University of Illinois commissioned several questions to be asked when the survey went into the field. The responses from these questions were not part of the published poll.

5. Ibid.

Chapter 1. The Changing Faces of Illinois

1. Terry Sanford, *Storm over the States* (New York: McGraw-Hill, 1967), p. 7.

2. *Go to 2040*, Chicago Metropolitan Agency for Planning, 2012. Civic groups such as the Metropolitan Planning Council and Metropolis Strategies have also been deeply involved in planning for and thinking about the Chicago region.

3. This brief historical treatment draws heavily on James D. Nowlan, Samuel K. Gove, and Richard J. Winkel Jr., *Illinois Politics: A Citizen's Guide* (Urbana: University of Illinois Press, 2009), chap. 1.

4. Robert M. Sutton, "The Politics of Regionalism Nineteenth Century Style," in *Diversity, Conflict, and State Politics: Regionalism in Illinois*, ed. Peter F. Nardulli (Urbana: University of Illinois Press, 1989), 97; Robert P. Howard, *Illinois: A History of the Prairie State* (Grand Rapids, MI: Eerdmans, 1972).

5. Howard, *Illinois: A History*, p. 130.

6. Ibid., pp. 306–7. As late as the Civil War, Illinois was passing propositions that prohibited Negroes from migrating into the state and denied them the right to vote and to hold office.

7. Cullom Davis, "Illinois: Crossroads and Cross Section," in *Heartland: Comparative Histories of the Midwestern States*, ed. James H. Madison (Bloomington: Indiana University Press, 1988), p. 133.

8. For a good discussion of the internal improvements effort, see Howard, *Illinois: A History*, chap. 9.

9. Richard J. Jensen, *Illinois: A Bicentennial History* (New York: Norton, 1978), chap. 2.

10. Ibid., p. 86.

11. For excellent discussion of the settlement of Illinois see Frederick M. Wirt, "The Changing Social Bases of Regionalism: People, Cultures, and Politics in Illinois," in *Diversity, Conflict*, ed. Nardulli, p. 31, and Davis, "Illinois: Crossroads."

12. James Simeone, *Democracy and Slavery in Frontier Illinois* (DeKalb: Northern Illinois University Press, 2000).

13. Jensen, *Illinois: A Bicentennial History*, chap. 2.

14. Ibid., pp. 52–53.

15. Ibid., pp. 53–54.

16. Ibid., p. 49.

17. William Cronon, *Nature's Metropolis: Chicago and the Great West* (New York: Norton, 1991), chap. 8.

18. Kristina Valaitis, "Understanding Illinois," *Texas Journal* 14 (Fall–Winter 1992): 20–22.

19. Cronon, *Nature's Metropolis*, pp. 208–9.

20. Ibid., chap. 7, "The Busy Hive," provides an assessment of the business dynamics of Chicago and the Midwest.

21. As cited in ibid., p. 3, from Frank Norris, *The Pit* (New York: Doubleday, 1903).

22. Howard, *Illinois: A History*, chap. 21.

23. Cronon, *Nature's Metropolis*, p. 347. A few years after the 1893 fair, architect Daniel Burnham designed "The Chicago Plan," a city of wide boulevards,

spacious parks, and an unobstructed lakefront. Much of the audacious plan was implemented.

24. Jensen, *Illinois: A Bicentennial History*, p. 162.

25. Nelson Algren, *Chicago: City on the Make* (New York: McGraw Hill,, 1951), p. 56.

26. From Adele Simmons, "A Global City," in *Twenty-First Century Chicago*, ed. Dick Simpson and Constance A. Mixon (San Diego: Cognella, 2012), p. 153.

27. Howard, *Illinois: A History*, pp. 554–55.

28. "Chicago Devises Master Plan to Better Compete in 2040," *New York Times*, July 18, 2010, p. 23B.

29. U.S. Census Bureau, State and County QuickFacts, http://quickfacts.census .gov/qfd/states/17000.html; Illinois Population Trends 2000 to 2030, Department of Commerce and Economic Opportunity, Springfield, Illinois, 2005.

30. See Cheng H. Chiang and Richard Kolhauser, "Who Are We? Illinois' Changing Population," *Illinois Issues*, December 1982, pp. 6–8. Also, thanks to Sue Ebitsch of the Illinois Department of Commerce and Economic Opportunity for sharing data from various Census reports. The estimates are those of the authors, based on this article and the shared data.

31. U.S. Census Bureau, http://quickfacts.census.gov/qfd/states/17000.html; Chiang and Kolhauser, "Who Are We?" pp. 6–8; Maureen Foertsch McKinney, "Census Reveals Surge in Latino Residents," *Illinois Issues*, April 2011, p. 14.

32. Interactive Illinois Report Card, http://www.isbe.net/assessment/report _card.htm.

33. Huffington Post, "Chicago Population Growth," http://www.huffingtonpost .com/2013/05/23/chicago-population-growth_n_3327135.html.

34. Norman Walzer and Brian L. Harger, "The Rural Midwest: How Is It Faring?" *Rural Research Report*, vol. 23, no. 1, Illinois Institute for Rural Affairs, Western Illinois University, Macomb, Fall 2012, p. 2.

35. Matthew Hall, "Lessons Learned from the 2010 Census," Illinois Report 2012, Institute of Government and Public Affairs, University of Illinois, Urbana, 2012, p. 11.

36. James D. Nowlan, *Illinois: Problems and Promise* (Galesburg: Illinois Public Policy Press, 1986); J. Fred Giertz, email correspondence with Jim Nowlan, July 13, 2011; Kathleen O'Leary Morgan and Scott Morgan, *State Rankings 2009* (Washington, DC: CQ, 2009), p. 100.

37. Bureau of Economic Analysis, http://bea.gov/scb/pdf/2011/07%20July/0711 _gdp-state.pdf.

38. Frank Beal, "Investing in Chicago: Toward a Regional Agenda for Economic Growth," Metropolis Strategies, Chicago, 2011.

39. Geoffrey Hewings, Regional Economics Applications Laboratory, University of Illinois. www.real.illinois.edu.

40. U.S. Bureau of the Census, http://quickfacts.census.gov/qfd/states/17/17097 .html.

41. Nowlan, "Illinois Is in a Funk," *Kankakee Daily Journal*, May 18, 2011.

42. Illinois Policy Survey 2011, Center for Governmental Studies, Northern Illinois University, DeKalb, 2011.

43. Charles W. Leonard, "Results and Analysis of the Third Annual Simon Poll: A Statewide Survey of Illinois Voters, Fall 2010," Paul Simon Public Policy Institute, Southern Illinois University, Carbondale, 2011.

44. John S. Jackson and Charles W. Leonard, "The Climate of Opinion in Southern Illinois: Continuity and Change," Paul Simon Public Policy Institute, Southern Illinois University, Carbondale, 2011.

45. "Illinois Residents See Broad Corruption in State Government and Seek Action for Change," study conducted by Belden Russonello & Stewart, Washington, DC, January 2009.

46. "Americans Love Hawaii, Dislike California," Public Policy Polling, Raleigh, NC, from a press release, February 21, 2012.

47. Randy Erford, *Illinois State Spending: The Thompson Years, 1978–88* (Springfield: Taxpayers' Federation of Illinois, 1989), p. 22; Illinois Department of Human Services, Springfield.

48. Erford, *Illinois State Spending*, p. 1; Illinois State Budget 2012, http://cgfa .ilga.gov/upload/fy2012budgetsummary.pdf

49. Transportation for Illinois Coalition. http://tficillinois.org.

50. This is according to the "Airport Connectivity Quality Index" developed by the Massachusetts Institute of Technology Center for Air Transportation, as reported in *Crain's Chicago Business*, October 14, 2013, p. 2.

51. Kathleen O'Leary Morgan and Scott Morgan, *State Rankings 2013* (Washington, DC: CQ), p. 152.

52. Paul Merrion, "Chicago among World's Top 10 Business Hot Spots," *Crain's Chicago Business*, June 5, 2013.

Chapter 2. Fixing Past Budgeting Sins

1. Executive Budget for Fiscal Year 2014, Governor's Office of Management and Budget, Springfield, 2013, pp. 2–60–61, 2–64.

2. Traditional Budgetary Financial Report 2012, Illinois Office of the Comptroller, Springfield. http://www.ioc.state.il.us/index.cfm/resources/reports/traditional-budgetary-financial/.

3. Calculations by Mike Klemens for the Taxpayers' Federation of Illinois, Springfield, October 2013.

4. Traditional Budgetary Financial Report 2012, Illinois Office of the Comptroller, Springfield.

5. "Pocket Guide to the Illinois State Budget, 2009," Illinois Tax Foundation, Springfield, 2009. Source: Illinois State Budget, various years.

6. Patrick O'Grady, "Taxes and Distributions by Region of the State," Legislative Research Unit, Illinois General Assembly, Springfield, March 9, 1989.

7. Kurt Fowler, "State Government: A Major Funder of Local Governments." *Tax Facts* 64, no. 6 (November/December 2011), Taxpayers' Federation of Illinois, Springfield.

8. For a more comprehensive discussion of budgeting in Illinois, see James D. Nowlan, Samuel K. Gove, and Richard J. Winkel Jr., *Illinois Politics: A Citizen's Guide* (Urbana: University of Illinois Press, 2010), chap. 10, "Taxing and Spending."

9. Robert Mandeville, "It's the Same Old Song," in *Illinois State Budget, Fiscal Year 1991* (Springfield: Office of the Governor, March 1990), pp. 1–14.

10. David Vaught, speech to the 2012 Downstate Summit in Decatur, IL, sponsored by the East Central Illinois Economic Development Council at Lakeland College, Mattoon, IL, September 20, 2012.

11. Richard F. Dye, Nancy W. Hudspeth, and David Merriman, "IGPA Fiscal Futures Model," Institute of Government and Public Affairs, Urbana, October 2013. http://igpa.uillinois.edu/system/files/Fiscal-Futures-Projections-Oct-2013.pdf.

12. Ibid.

13. For a good discussion of structural deficits, see Richard F. Dye, Nancy W. Hudspeth, and Daniel P. McMillen, "Fiscal Condition Critical: The Budget Crisis in Illinois," in the *Illinois Report 2010*, Institute of Government and Public Affairs, University of Illinois, Urbana, 2010, pp. 17–18.

14. Richard Dye, Nancy Hudspeth, and David Merriman, "Fact Sheet: Peering Over Illinois' Fiscal Cliff: New Projections from IGPA's Fiscal Futures Model," Institute of Government and Public Affairs, University of Illinois, Chicago, October 2013. See igpa.uillinois.edu/fiscalfutures for the full report.

15. Charles Leonard, Ryan P. Burge, and Emily S. Carroll, "The Movement of Opinion Toward Spending Cuts," The Simon Review, Paper no. 27, Paul Simon Public Policy Institute, Southern Illinois University, Carbondale, January 2012, p. 32.

16. For a thorough discussion of the history of the budget crisis, see "The State Fiscal Crisis: How Did We Get Here?" in *Fiscal Facts* (Springfield: Office of the Illinois Comptroller, September 2011), pp. 4–12.

17. Kurt Fowler, "Another View of Crowding Out," *Tax Facts* 65, no. 4 (July/ August 2012), Taxpayers' Federation of Illinois, Springfield, p. 6.

18. Julie Hamos, director of the Illinois Department of Healthcare and Family Services, interview with Jim Nowlan, Springfield, May 3, 2013.

19. Robert Kaestner and Nicole Kazee, "Health Care Reform and Medicaid: Covering the Uninsured," *The Illinois Report 2011*, Institute of Government and Public Affairs, University of Illinois, Urbana, 2011, p. 61.

20. State Healthcare Statistics, Kaiser Family Foundation. kff.org/medicaid/state-indicator/growth-in-medicaid-spending-fy90-fy10/?state=IL.

21. Dye, Hudspeth, and Merriman, "Through a Dark Glass," pp. 42–52.

22. Christopher Johnston, interview with Jim Nowlan, Indianapolis, July 18, 2012.

23. Ibid.

24. Matthew Walberg and Joe Mahr, "Tribune Analysis: Average Raise in 2009–2010 for CEOs of 18 Nonprofits Double That for Private-Industry Workers," *Chicago Tribune*, June 21, 2012.

25. *Fee Imposition Report 2012*, Office of the Illinois Comptroller, Springfield, 2012, p. 1.

26. Ibid., p. 12.

27. The Tax Foundation, "About Us," http://www.taxfoundation.org/about-us.

28. *Tax Expenditure Report, Fiscal Year 2011*, Illinois Office of the Comptroller, Springfield. www.illinoiscomptroller.com.

29. "Charting Progress Toward a More Efficient Regional and State Tax System via Indicators," Chicago Metropolitan Agency for Planning, July 18, 2013.

30. For a comprehensive discussion of the issue of a sales tax on services, see Benjamin L. Varner, "Service Taxes: 2011 Update," Commission on Governmental Forecasting and Accountability, Illinois General Assembly, Springfield, April 2011. http://cgfa.ilga.gov/Upload/ServiceTaxes2011update.pdf.

31. Therese McGuire, professor of public finance, Kellogg School of Management, telephone interview with Jim Nowlan, Northwestern University, November 25, 2013.

32. Rachel Wells, "Taxing Services: An Old Idea Re-emerges in the Face of Economic Peril," *Illinois Issues*, Springfield, http://illinoisissues.uis.edu/archives/2010/05/taxation.html.

33. Varner, "Service Taxes: 2011 Update," pp. 13–14. http://cgfa.ilga.gov/Upload/ServiceTaxes2011update.pdf.

34. Ryan Aprill, "Is Taxing Food All That Regressive?" Illinois Fiscal Policy Council Research Report #6, 2010, Springfield, pp. 1–6.

Chapter 3. Upgrading Education

1. Figures in this paragraph are from the Web sites of the Illinois State Board of Education (www.isbe.state.il.us/) and the Illinois Board of Higher Education (www.ibhe.org). The first section of this chapter draws heavily on James D. Nowlan, Samuel K. Gove, and Richard J. Winkel Jr., *Illinois Politics: A Citizen's Guide* (Urbana: University of Illinois Press, 2010), chap. 9, and citations therein.

2. Kathleen O'Leary Morgan and Scott Morgan, *State Rankings, 2013* (Los Angeles: CQ, 2013), p. 140.

3. Peter Mulhall, "Illinois K–12 Education," in *The Illinois Report 2007* (Urbana: Institute of Government and Public Affairs, University of Illinois, 2007), pp. 24–29.

4. Illinois State Board of Education, *Education Quickstats 2012*, http://www.isbe.net/research/pdfs/quickstats_2012.pdf.

5. Ibid.

6. Archdiocese of Chicago Board of Catholic Schools, "Strategic Plan for Catholic Schools, 2013–2016," http://gallery.mailchimp.com/a09fbf4d2497886d386e21d4b/files/StrategicPlanforCatholicSchools2_W7_4_.pdf

7. National Center for Education Statistics, Digest of Education Statistics, Table 40: Number and Percentage of Homeschooled Students Ages 5 through 17, 2012. http://nces.ed.gov/programs/digest/d11/tables/dt11_040.asp.

8. "Homeschool Statistics," *Let's Home School*, www.letshomeschool.com/articles39.html.

9. For an excellent discussion of education in Illinois before 1975, see Martin Burlingame, "Politics and Policies of Elementary and Secondary Education," in *Illinois: Political Processes and Government Performance*, ed. Edgar Crane (Dubuque, Iowa: Kendall-Hunt, 1980), pp. 370–89. See also Cullom Davis, "Illinois Crossroads and Cross Section," in *Heartland: Comparative Histories of the Midwestern States*, ed. James H. Madison (Bloomington: Indiana University Press, 1988), p. 154.

10. Advance Illinois, "The State We're in 2012: A Report Card on Public Education in Illinois," 2012, p. 7, citing as its source National Center for Education Statistics, *National Assessment of Educational Progress, 2003–2011*, http://nces.ed.gov/nationsreportcard/about/.

11. Stephen Olemacher, "Early Presidential Primary States Are Far from U.S. Average," Associated Press, Washington, DC, May 17, 2007.

12. Advance Illinois, "State We're in 2012," p. 20.

13. Amy M. Hightower, "States Show Spotty Progress Across Swath of Education Gauges," *Education Week*, January 10, 2013, pp. 42–52.

14. Illinois Policy Survey, Center for Governmental Studies, Northern Illinois University, DeKalb, 2012, p. 13.

15. Advance Illinois, "State We're in 2012," p. 24

16. Ibid.

17. Illinois State Board of Education. http://www.isbe.net/reports/annual12/resources.pdf.

18. NEA Research, "Rankings & Estimates: Rankings of the States 2012 and Estimates of School Statistics 2013," National Education Association, December 2012, p. 42. Illinois actually would fare somewhat better in terms of state support for education if the Illinois Personal Property Replacement Tax were considered a state tax, which it is, rather than a local source of revenue, which the ISBE considers it. The tax of 2.5 percent on corporation income was established in 1979 to replace local government revenues lost by the abolition of the personal property tax. In 2011 the state Personal Property Replacement Tax generated $1.38 billion for local governments, and about $856 million, or 62 percent, went to school districts. This would have increased the state contribution to local schools by about 2 percent of the total and reduced the local contribution by about the same percentage. Illinois would still rank among the bottom ten states in terms of state support for public education as a percentage of total funding.

19. See Nowlan, Gove, and Winkel, chap. 9, for a discussion of state funding for local school districts.

20. *Report of the State Budget Crisis Task Force: Illinois Report* (New York: State Budget Crisis Task Force, 2012), p. 39.

21. Ibid.

22. "Is School Funding Fair? A National Report Card," 2d ed., Education Law Center, Rutgers Graduate School of Education, New Brunswick NJ, 2012. www .schoolfundingfairness.org/National_Report _Card_2012.pdf.

23. "Illinois Education Funding Recommendations," Illinois Education Funding Advisory Board, January 2011, http://www.isbe.net/efab/pdf/final_report_1:11.pdf.

24. The discussion of the school aid formula benefits from various sources provided by the ISBE Web site. In addition, during his work for the Taxpayers' Accountability Board and then the Taxpayers' Federation of Illinois in 2009–10, Ted Dabrowski became an expert on school funding in Illinois. The authors have benefited from many discussions with Mr. Dabrowski.

25. All the figures in this discussion of school funding are from the ISBE, some as reported in an internal paper by staff for the Republicans in the State Senate, which was provided to the authors.

26. James D. Nowlan, *A New Game Plan for Illinois* (Chicago: Neltnor House, 1989), chap. 4.

27. Randy Fritz, teacher in the Williamsfield, IL, school district, in discussions with Jim Nowlan, undated.

28. As reported by Jim Broadway, State School News Service, Springfield, Illinois, April 5, 2011.

29. Ibid.

30. Benjamin Superfine, Marl A. Smylie, Steven Tozer, and David Mayrowetz, "Promising Strategies for Improving K–12 Education in Illinois: Improving the Educator Workforce," in *Illinois Report 2009*, Institute of Government and Public Affairs, University of Illinois, Urbana, 2009, pp. 50–64.

31. "Education Report: Education for the Future in Northeast Illinois," Chicago Community Trust, 2010, p. 33.

32. In 2011, the first year for which test scores were reported, Quest students scored 14 points higher than the Peoria district average and 2 points better (79 versus 77) than the statewide average. See Illinois State Board of Education, State Report Card, http://www.illinoisreportcard.com/.

33. "The Evaluation of Charter School Impacts: Final Report," Institute for Education Sciences, National Center for Educational Evaluation and Regional Assistance, U.S. Department of Education, Washington, DC, 2010, p. xvii.

34. Ibid., p. xvii.

35. "Charting a Better Course," *Economist*, July 7, 2012, pp. 29–30.

36. Jay Mathews, "Study Says KIPP Student Gains Substantial," *Washington Post*, March 3, 2013.

37. Andrew J. Rotherham, "KIPP Schools: A Reform Triumph, or Disappointment?" *Time*, April 27, 2011.

38. Jeff Burger, deputy state school superintendent for Iowa, telephone interview with Jim Nowlan, August 19, 2013.

39. Stanley O. Ikenberry, Daniel T. Layzell, and W. Randall Kangas, "Higher Education and Illinois' Future," in *Illinois Report 2008*, Institute of Government and Public Affairs, University of Illinois, Urbana, 2008, p. 71.

40. "Preliminary Fall 2012 Enrollments in Illinois Higher Education," ISBE, Springfield, February 2013.

41. "Completing College: A State-Level View of Student Attainment Rates," National Student Clearinghouse Research Center, Herndon, VA, 2012. This statistic is for "six-year outcomes for students who started at four-year public institutions (in 2006), by origin state."

42. As reported in Harry Berman and Stacy Reed, "Springfield's Continuum of Learning: A Model Initiative to Increase Educational Attainment in Illinois," in *Illinois Report 2011*, Institute of Government and Public Affairs, University of Illinois, Urbana, 2011, p. 106.

43. Illinois Board of Higher Education, Springfield, 2011. http://www.ibhe.org/Fiscal%20Affairs/PDF/FY2013BudgetAppropriations.pdf.

44. "Institutional Profiles," ISBE, Springfield, 2012.

45. Sandy Baum and Patricia Steele, "Who Borrows Most? Bachelor's Degree Recipients with High Levels of Student Debt," *Trends in Higher Education Series: 2010* (Washington, DC: College Board, 2010). www.collegeboard.com/trends.

46. Ray Schroeder, associate vice chancellor for online learning, University of Illinois, in discussion with Jim Nowlan, Springfield, January 7, 2013.

47. Ibid.

Chapter 4. Improving Human Services and Health Care

1. Robert F. Rich, "The Future of Medicaid," presentation to the Union League Club of Chicago, September 5, 2011.

2. A partial list of additional services provided and the numbers of people served by the state can be found in the Illinois State Budget 2013 under the Department of Human Services.

3. *Illinois State Budget 2014*, Governor's Office of Management and Budget, Springfield.

4. State Representative David Leitch, interview with Jim Nowlan, Peoria, January 3, 2012.

5. *Report of the Taxpayers' Action Board* (known as the TAB Report), Office of the Governor, Springfield, March 2010, pp. 19–20.

6. *Five Year Medical Assistance Budget Outlook*, Illinois Department of Healthcare and Family Services, Springfield, no date.

7. http://www.economist.com/blogs/dailychart/2011/08/americas-fiscal-union.

8. Nana Mkheidze, "Federal Medical Assistance Plan (FMAP): Is Illinois Treated Fairly?" *Tax Facts*, Taxpayers' Federation of Illinois, Springfield, November-December 2012, pp. 5–12.

9. Ibid.

10. J. Fred Giertz, "Commentary on the Illinois Economy," paper at the Institute of Government and Public Affairs, University of Illinois, Urbana, July 28, 2005; State Rankings, 2013, p. 98.

11. TAB Report, p. 27.

12. Illinois must also ensure that only those eligible for Medicaid benefits are actually enrolled. There is a strong feeling among some legislators that thousands of persons actively enrolled in the Illinois Medicaid program are ineligible because of lack of permanent residency in Illinois or because of income that is too high. In 2012 the legislature directed HFS to conduct a review of all those enrolled and to purge those found to be ineligible. This effort has been stalled because public employee unions have challenged in court the outsourcing of the eligibility review to a private contractor rather than giving the task to state workers.

13. Judith Graham, "Illinois Medicaid's managed care effort stumbles," *Chicago Tribune*, August 26, 2011.

14. State Health Facts, Kaiser Family Foundation, kff.org/Medicaid/state-indi-cator/growthinmedicaidspending-fy90-fy10/paymentsperenrollee-fy2009.

15. John C. Goodman, "Should We Replace Medicaid with Block Grants to States?" *Psychology Today*, January 2, 2013. http://www.psychologytoday.com/blog/curing-the-healthcare-crisis/201301/should-we-replace-medicaid-block-grants-states.

16. Interview by Jim Nowlan with John Tillman, Chicago, June 7, 2012.

17. *Budget Solutions 2013: Innovation for Illinois*, Illinois Policy Institute, Chicago, 2012, pp. 23–33.

18. "Medicaid Expansion Through Premium Assistance: Fact Sheet," Kaiser Commission on Medicaid and the Uninsured, July 2013, pp. 1–4.

19. AFSCME Council 31's Health Improvement Plan Strategy and Platform, PowerPoint presentation by Hank Scheff of AFSCME Council 31, February 24, 2011.

20. Ezekiel J. Emanuel, "Health Care's Good News," *New York Times*, February 15, 2013, p. A23.

21. Taxpayer Accountability Board, "Reverse the Bias Toward Institutional Care in the Long-term Care System," Office of the Governor, 2010, p. 36.

22. Debra Matlock, deputy director, Illinois Department of Children and Family Services, interview with Jim Nowlan, Chicago, January 14, 2012.

23. Robert Kaestner and Anthony Lo Sasso, "Public Policies to Increase Hospital Competition, Improve Quality of Inpatient Care and Lower Health Care Costs," *The Illinois Report 2013*, Institute of Government and Public Affairs, University of Illinois, Urbana, 2013, pp. 61–67.

24. Don Moss, interview with Jim Nowlan, Springfield, December 30, 2011.

25. See, e.g., *Colbert v. Quinn* (No. 07 C 4737, in the United States District Court for the Northern District of Illinois, filed 2007) and *Ligas v. Hamos* (Case: 1:05-cv-04331 Document #549, filed 2005).

Chapter 5. Economic Development for Stability

1. *CNN Money*. http://money.cnn.com/interactive/economy/state-unemploy-ment-rates.

2. Regional Economics Applications Laboratory, University of Illinois. www.real.illinois.edu.

3. Steve McClure, interview with James Nowlan, Springfield, January 5, 2011.

4. Jamey Dunn, "All About Business," *Illinois Issues*, November 2011, p. 26.

5. See *Rich States, Poor States: ALEC-Laffer State Economic Competitiveness Index* (Washington, D.C.: American Legislative Exchange Council, 2012) for the

ALEC ranking; http://chiefexecutive.net/best-worst-states-for-business-2013 for the *CEO* magazine ranking; John Pletz, "Illinois Among Bottom 3 States for Business: Survey," *Crain's Chicago Business*, September 19, 2011, for the DCI ranking; http://www.forbes.com/best-states-for-business/#page:4_sort:0_direction:asc_search for the Forbes ranking; Scott Drenkard and Joseph Henchman, *2013 State Business Tax Climate Index*, Tax Foundation, Washington, DC, October 2012, no. 64, p. 3, and earlier editions (http://taxfoundation.org/article/2014-state-business-tax-climate-index) for the Tax Foundation ranking; http://www.cnbc.com/id/100817171 for the CNBC ranking; and http://www.sbecouncil.org/2011/12/02/positive-lessons-from-and-for-the-states/ for the Small Business and Entrepreneurship Council ranking.

6. Joseph Cortright and Heike Mayer, "Increasingly Rank: The Use and Misuse of Rankings in Economic Development," *Economic Development Quarterly* 18, no. 1 (February 2004): pp. 34–39.

7. Peter Fisher, *Grading Places: What Do the Business Climate Rankings Really Tell Us?* Economic Policy Institute, Washington, D.C., 2005, back cover.

8. Survey of members of the Illinois Development Council, September–October 2011, by James Nowlan.

9. Oregon Department of Consumer and Business Services, "Workers' Compensation Rates, State-by-State Comparison, 2010," https://data.oregon.gov/Business/Workers-Compensation-Rates-State-by-State-Comparis/fqmb-yv95.

10. Ibid.

11. "The Impact of Judicial Activism in Illinois: Workers' Compensation Rulings from the Employer's Perspective," Illinois Chamber of Commerce, Chicago, 2013.

12. Ibid. See also *Chicago Tribune*, August 13, 2013, p. 14.

13. Beth Hundsdorfer and George Pawlaczyk, "Lawmakers Call for Review of Workers' Comp Claims by Prison Guards, Arbitrators," *Belleville (IL) News-Democrat*, February 10, 2011.

14. Claudio Agostini and Soraphol Tulayasathien, "Tax Effects on Investment Location: Evidence of Foreign Direct Investment in the United States," Office of Tax Policy Research, University of Michigan Business School, 2001, as reported in *2012 State Business Tax Climate Index*, Tax Foundation, Washington, DC, January 2012, p. 6.

15. J. William Harden and William H. Hoyt, "Do States Choose Their Mix of Taxes to Minimize Employment Losses?" *National Tax Journal*, March 2003, pp. 7–26, as reported in *2012 State Business Tax Climate Index*, Tax Foundation, Washington, DC, January 2012, p. 6.

16. "FY2013 Economic and Revenue Update and Preliminary FY2014 Revenue Outlook," Commission on Government Forecasting and Accountability, Illinois General Assembly, Springfield, 2012, p. 29.

17. "Just the Facts: A Primer on Illinois Pensions," Civic Committee of the Com-

mercial Club, Chicago, 2012; "Analysis of Change in State Pension Unfunded Liability—1985 Through 2012," Commission on Government Forecasting and Accountability, Springfield, 2013.

18. Therese J. McGuire, "Managing Economic Development in Times of Fiscal Uncertainty," presentation at the Federal Reserve Bank of Chicago, April 4, 2013.

19. Area Development Online, "Right-to-Work/Low-Union-Profile States," http://www.areadevelopment.com/laborEducation/November2012/RTW-union-profile-manufacturing-location-factors-2716141.shtml.

20. Ibid.

21. Eric Shields of the Indiana Economic Development Corporation, interview with James Nowlan, September 5, 2013.

22. Greg Hinz, "Trending: Special Report; A New City Is Rising in America—Downtown Chicago," *Crain's Chicago Business*, March 4, 2013.

23. Paul Merrion, "Chicago Among World's Top 10 Hot Spots," *Crain's Chicago Business*, June 5, 2013.

24. Frank Beal, interview with James Nowlan, May 12, 2011.

25. "A Plan for Economic Growth and Jobs," *World Business Chicago*, February 2012; "Go to 2040," Chicago Metropolitan Agency on Planning, 2011; "Restoring Chicago's Momentum," Metropolis Strategies, Chicago, 2011; "The Chicago Tri-State Metropolitan Area, United States," preliminary version, Organization for Economic and Cooperative Development, Paris, France, February 2012, produced for the Chicagoland Chamber of Commerce; "2012 Plan for Prosperity," Metropolitan Planning Council, Chicago, 2012.

26. Frank Beal, Emily Harris, and Tim Quayle, "Restoring Chicago's Momentum: A Regional Agenda for Economic Growth," Metropolis Strategies, Chicago, 2011.

27. "Chicago Tri-State Metropolitan Area," preliminary version, p. 19.

28. "Plan for Economic Growth," p. 28.

29. "Chicago Tri-State Metropolitan Area," preliminary version, p. 22.

30. Dylan Scott, "Gearing Up Down South," *Governing*, July 2012, pp. 54–57.

31. Ibid., p. 30.

32. Richard C. Longworth, *Caught in the Middle: America's Heartland in the Age of Globalism* (New York: Bloomsbury, 2008), p. 248.

33. Richard C. Longworth, "Milwaukee and Chicago Need Collaborative Effort," *Journal-Sentinel* (Milwaukee), July 7, 2012. http://www.jsonline.com/news/opinion/milwaukee-and-chicago-need-collaborative-effort-ov5vrni-161628985.html.

34. McClure interview.

35. Norman Walzer and Brian L. Harger, "The Rural Midwest: How Is It Faring?" *Rural Research Report*, 23, no. 1, Illinois Institute for Rural Affairs, Western Illinois University, Macomb, Fall 2012.

36. William deBuys, *A Great Aridness: Climate Change and the Future of the American Southwest* (Oxford: Oxford University Press, 2011), p. 159. See also Alex Prud'homme, *The Ripple Effect: The Fate of Freshwater in the Twenty-First Century* (New York: Scribner, 2011).

37. H. Allen Wehrmann, interview with James Nowlan, Champaign, June 26, 2011.

38. Steven G. Koven and Thomas S. Lyons, *Economic Development: Strategies for State and Local Practice*, 2d ed. (Washington, DC): ICMA, 2010, p. 259.

39. Aksh Gupta, "$150 Million for Sears? Here's a Different Idea," *Crain's Chicago Business*, February 27, 2012, p. 13.

40. William Fulton, "Economic Gardening in Michigan," *Governing*, July 2012, pp. 22–23.

41. Office of the Comptroller, *Fiscal Year 2010 Tax Expenditure Report*, August 2011, p. 5.

42. McGuire, "Managing Economic Development." The comments were made during her presentation.

43. Koven and Lyons, p. 121.

Chapter 6. Transportation: Maintaining Our Greatest Strength

1. "Proposed FY2012–2016 Public Transportation Improvement Program," Illinois Department of Transportation, Spring 2011, p. 3.

2. "Metropolitan Chicago's Freight Cluster: A Drill-Down Report on Infrastructure, Innovation, and Workforce," Chicago Metropolitan Agency for Planning, Summary Report, June 2012, p. 10.

3. "Transforming Transportation for Tomorrow: FY2013–2018 Proposed Multi-Modal Transportation Improvement Program," Illinois Department of Transportation, April 2012, p. 70.

4. "Illinois State Transportation Plan," Illinois Department of Transportation, 2007, p. 12.

5. "Illinois Highway Statistics Sheet 2011," Illinois Department of Transportation. http://www.dot.state.il.us.

6. This was computed as follows: with 16,000 miles of state roads, and given that the average road needs improvement every 20 years, IDOT should be improving 800 miles of road per year. According to "Transforming Transportation," p. 16, IDOT will repair 2,302 miles over six-year period, or 384 miles per year. Since roads wear out at average rate of 800 miles per year, state roads are now wearing out twice as fast as they are being repaired.

7. "Transforming Transportation," p. 19.

8. Ibid.

9. TRIP (a national transportation research group), "Key Facts About Illinois' Surface Transportation System and Federal Funding," Washington, DC, April 2012.

10. "On the Move: State Strategies for 21st Century Transportation Solutions," National Conference of State Legislatures, Denver, CO, July 2012.

11. "Illinois Highway and Street Mileage Statistics 2011," Illinois Department of Transportation, December 2011, p. 28.

12. Office of the Comptroller, Revenue Sources FY 2012. http://www.wh1.ioc .state.il.us/Expert/Rev/ERControl.cfm?Control=Rev&Reset=Y&GroupBy=None &SortName=No.

13. "For the Record, 2011," Illinois Department of Transportation, October 2011, pt. 2, p. 1.

14. Regional Transportation Authority, "Overview and History," http://www .rtachicago.com/initiatives/rtams.html.

15. These trip totals include the Chicago Transit Authority, Metropolitan Transportation Authority and Pace (suburban bus service). The data were assembled from 2012 budgets by Linda Wheeler, former policy and planning director for the Illinois Department of Transportation.

16. "RTA Capital Asset Condition Assessment," Regional Transportation Authority, 2010. http://www.rtachicago.com/images/stories/final_RTA_imgs/RTA%20 Asset%20Condition%20Assessment%20REPORT.pdf.

17. "2012 Summary Briefing of Final Operating Budgets, Two-Year Financial Plans and Five-Year Capital Programs of the RTA, Chicago Transit Authority (CTA), Metra and Pace," Regional Transportation Authority, December 2011, p. 31.

18. "2011 Annual Urban Mobility Report." Data from Performance Measure Summary, Chicago IL–IN, Texas Transportation Institute, September 2011.

19. "Go to 2040 Comprehensive Regional Plan," CMAP, October 2010, p. 308.

20. CREATE, "Overview." http://www.createprogram.org/about.htm.

21. City of Chicago, "About the O'Hare Modernization Program," http://www .cityofchicago.org/city/en/depts/doa/provdrs/omp/svcs/about_the_omp.html.

22. "Transforming Transportation," p. 19.

23. "The Freight-Manufacturing Nexus: Metropolitan Chicago's Built-in Advantage," Chicago Metropolitan Agency for Planning, August 2013.

24. "Illinois Travel Statistics 2011," Illinois Department of Transportation, 2012, p. 29.

25. Ibid.

26. Linda Wheeler, former director of policy and planning, Illinois Department of Transportation, interview with James Nowlan, Springfield, June 15, 2012.

27. Presentation to Government Affairs Workshop of American Council of Engineering Companies of Illinois, Transportation for Illinois Coalition, Chicago, June 2012.

28. Craig Fink, former president of the Illinois Association of County Engineers, telephone interview with James Nowlan, January 14, 2013.

29. "2012 Summary Briefing," p. 31.

30. Regional Transportation Authority, "System Ridership," http://www.rtams .org/rtams/systemRidership.jsp.

31. "Moving Beyond Congestion," Regional Transportation Authority, 2007, n.p.

32. "Moving at the Speed of Congestion," Metropolitan Planning Council, August 2008.

33. "2012 Annual Urban Mobility Report," Texas Transportation Institute, College Station, Texas, p. 24.

34. Ibid., p. 50.

35. "Freight Condition Index Rating, 2010," American Transportation Research Institute and Federal Highway Administration, October 2011.

36. CREATE Rail Operations Benefits Summary, http://www.createprogram .org/benefits.htm.

37. These data come from the Office of the Comptroller, http://www.ioc.state .il.us.

38. Larry Ehl, "How Much Is Your State Gas Tax Shrinking?" *Transportation Issues Daily*, January 31, 2012. http://www.transportationissuesdaily.com/how-much-is-your-state-gas-tax-shrinking/. The article links to the full history of twenty-six states' gas tax rates by the Institute on Taxation and Economic Policy.

39. This analysis is based on data from the Office of the Comptroller and provided to the authors by Linda Wheeler, former director of policy and planning for the Illinois Department of Transportation, Springfield.

40. "User Fee Revenues and Their Uses," Transportation for Illinois Coalition, Fall 2011, as provided to the authors by Linda Wheeler.

41. "Proposed Improvements for Illinois Highways for FY1999 Through the Present," Illinois Department of Transportation, as provided by Linda Wheeler.

42. Linda Wheeler, interview with James Nowlan, July 18, 2012.

43. "Illinois State Transportation Plan; Special Report: Transportation Funding," Illinois Department of Transportation, July 2007; "Capital Asset Condition Assessment," Regional Transportation Authority; "Move Illinois—Capital Program Summary," Illinois Toll Highway Authority.

44. "Highway Statistics Series, Table MF-205," as of December 2010. U.S. Department of Transportation, Federal Highway Administration,

45. "Oregon's Mileage Fee Concept and Road User Fee Pilot Program: Final Report," Oregon Department of Transportation, November 2007.

46. "Illinois Travel Statistics 2011," p. 34.

47. Mark Crawford, "Public-Private Partnerships (PPPs) Can Define a Community," *Area Development* (Westbury, NY), August 2012, p. 53.

48. Amtrak Fact Sheet, Fiscal Year 2012, State of Illinois, http://www.amtrak.com/pdf/factsheets/ILLINOIS12.pdf.

49. Ibid.

50. Ibid.

51. "Final Round of Hearings Scheduled," *State Journal-Register* (Springfield, IL), July 31, 2012.

52. "Chicago–St. Louis High-Speed Rail Tier 1 DEIS," Illinois Department of Transportation, July 2012, p. 3–63.

53. Ibid., p. 3–16.

54. Ibid., p. 3–20.

55. Ibid., p. 3–16

56. Ibid., p. 3–21.

57. "Go to 2040 Comprehensive Regional Plan," p. 292.

Chapter 7. Reengineering Our Governments

1. William G. Holland, "Management Audit of the State's Financial Reporting Systems," Office of the Auditor General, February 2011, p. iii.

2. Fred Montgomery, letter to James Nowlan, August 12, 2013.

3. Holland, "Management Audit," p. 165.

4. Ibid., p. 79.

5. Ibid.

6. Tom Shaer, telephone conversation with James Nowlan, September 16, 2013.

7. David Ormsby, The Illinois Observer, November 19, 2013. http://www.illinoisobserver.net.

8. "Statistical Section," Comprehensive Annual Financial Report 2012, Office of the Comptroller, Springfield, p. 328, and earlier years of the report, same section.

9. Robert Powers, telephone conversation with James Nowlan, September 3, 2013.

10. "Taxpayers' Action Board Report" [hereafter "TAB Report"], Office of the Governor, Springfield, 2010, pp. 94–104.

11. For a comprehensive overview of local governments in Illinois, see Robert F. Rich et al., "Multiplicity of Governments; Paucity of Money," Institute of Government and Public Affairs, University of Illinois, Urbana, 2010.

12. Kathleen O'Leary Morgan and Scott Morgan, *State Rankings 2013* (Washington, DC: CQ), p. 366.

13. Christopher Berry, *Imperfect Union: Representation and Taxation in Multilevel Governments* (New York: Cambridge University Press, 2009).

14. Ann Lousin, discussion with James Nowlan, September 10, 2013.

15. Quarterly Report, Illinois Department of Corrections, April 1, 2013.

16. "State of Recidivism: The Revolving Door of America's Prisons," Pew Center on the States, Washington, DC, April 2011, p. 14.

17. "TAB Report," p. 85.

18. "Adult Redeploy Illinois: 2012 Annual Report to the Governor and General Assembly on the Implementation and Projected Impact," Adult Redeploy Illinois Oversight Board, March 8, 2013, p. 1.

19. "TAB Report," p. 85.

20. Ibid., p. 90.

21. Public Labor Relations Act, Connecticut General Statutes Sec. 5–278(b).

Chapter 8. Corruption in Illinois: An Enduring Tradition

1. For purposes of our discussion, we define *corruption* as any personal gain at public expense.

2. Ninian Wirt Edwards, *History of Illinois from 1778 to 1833; and the Life and Times of Ninian Edwards* (Springfield: n.p., 1870), p. 21.

3. Ibid.

4. James L. Merriner, *Grafters and Goo Goos: Corruption and Reform in Chicago, 1833–2003* (Carbondale: Southern Illinois University Press, 2004), p. 44. This book provides a well-written, comprehensive overview of corruption in Chicago and of efforts to combat it.

5. Robert J. Schoenberg, *Mr. Capone* (New York: William Morrow, 1992), p. 40.

6. Ibid.; James D. Nowlan, *Glory, Darkness, Light: A History of the Union League Club of Chicago* (Evanston: Northwestern University Press, 2005), p. 41.

7. Ibid.

8. Ibid., chap. 7, "The Buying of a U.S. Senate Seat—as Revealed at the Union League Club," p. 73.

9. Schoenberg, *Mr. Capone*, p. 40.

10. Ibid.

11. Ibid., p. 41.

12. Merriner, *Grafters and Goo Goos,* p. 116.

13. Kenneth Alsop, *The Bootleggers* (New Rochelle, NY: Arlington House, 1961), p. 239.

14. Schoenberg, *Mr. Capone*, p. 41.

15. Ibid.

16. Robert P. Howard, *Illinois: A History of the Prairie State* (Grand Rapids: Eerdmans, 1972), pp. 549–50.

17. Kenneth A. Manaster, *Illinois Justice: The Scandal of 1969 and the Rise of John Paul Stevens* (Chicago: University of Chicago Press, 2001), generally.

18. Howard, *Illinois: A History of the Prairie State*, p. 563.

19. James D. Nowlan, Samuel K. Gove and Richard J. Winkel, *Illinois Politics: A Citizen's Guide* (Urbana: University of Illinois Press, 2010), pp. 143–44. See James Tuohy and Rob Warden, *Greylord: Justice, Chicago Style* (New York: Putnam's, 1989), and Robert Cooley with Hillel Levin, *When Corruption Was King* (New York: Carroll and Graf, 2004) for gripping accounts of Operation Greylord and Operation Gambat, respectively.

20. Thomas J. Gradel, Dick Simpson, and Andris Zimelis, "Curing Corruption in Illinois: Anti-Corruption Report Number 1," University of Illinois at Chicago Department of Political Science, February 3, 2009, p. 5.

21. Greg Hinz, "Blagojevich Fund-Raiser Rezko Indicted," October 11, 2006, http://www.chicagobusiness.com/article/20061011/NEWS/200022406/blagojevich-fund-raiser-rezko-indicted.

22. Ibid.

23. Jeff Coen and John Chase, "Golden: How Rod Blagojevich Talked Himself out of the Governor's Office and into Prison," manuscript from Chicago Review Press, May 24, 2012.

24. "Corruption on Parade," *Chicago Tribune*, January 22, 2006.

25. Dick Simpson, James Nowlan et al., *Chicago and Illinois: Leading the Pack in Corruption*, University of Illinois at Chicago Department of Political Science, February 15, 2012, table 2.

26. Ibid., table 1.

27. Jason Grotto and Ray Long, "Ex-Lawmaker Nearly Doubles His Pension with One Month of Work," *Chicago Tribune*, December 16, 2011. http://articles.chicagotribune.com/2011–12–16/news/ct-met-pension-molaro-20111216_1_pension-fund-pension-crisis-public-pension.

28. Richard Winters, "Unique or Typical? Political Corruption in the American States . . . and Illinois," paper presented at the Ethics and Reform Symposium on Illinois Government, September 27–28, 2012, and available from the Paul Simon Public Policy Institute, Southern Illinois University, Carbondale.

29. Illinois Integrity Initiative Survey, Institute of Government and Public Affairs, University of Illinois, Urbana, December 2011. Survey was taken for the Initiative by Kelton Research, New York, New York and Culver City, California.

30. Richard T. Boylan and Cheryl X. Long, "Measuring Public Corruption in the American States," *State Politics and Policy Quarterly*, 3 (2003): 420–38.

31. Illinois Integrity Initiative Survey.

32. Survey by Jim Nowlan of the members of the Illinois Development Council, May 2011. Two hundred surveys went out via Survey Monkey; seventy responses were received.

33. Dick Simpson and Melissa Zmuda, "Corruption in Illinois," paper presented at the conference "Is There a Culture of Corruption in Illinois?" Institute of Government and Public Affairs of the University of Illinois, Chicago, March 2, 2012.

34. Lilliard Richardson, "Political Corruption and Its Effect on Civic Involvement," paper presented at the Ethics and Reform Symposium, September 27–28, 2012, Chicago, and available from the Paul Simon Public Policy Institute at Southern Illinois University, Carbondale, p. 13.

35. Simpson and Zmuda, "Corruption in Illinois."

36. Daniel Elazar, "Political Culture of the United States," http://academic.regis .edu/jriley/421elazar.htm.

37. Michael Josephson, address at the Ethics and Reform Symposium held September 27–28, 2012, Chicago, sponsored by and remarks available from the Paul Simon Public Policy Institute, Southern Illinois University, Carbondale.

38. The exercise is as follows: Your brother has just been charged with a serious DUI. He will lose his license if convicted. He is in his first job after college and he absolutely must have a car to do his job. His wife is at home, pregnant with their first child.

The brother has employed a veteran lawyer. The lawyer says that he knows his way around the court system and that if your brother will provide him $1,000 in cash beyond his fee, he is confident he can have the charge dismissed.

Your brother turns to you for guidance. Should he:

- Go for it
- Reject the idea

39. Susan Rose-Ackerman, *Corruption and Government: Causes, Consequences, and Reform* (Cambridge: Cambridge University Press, 1999).

40. Charles Snyder, email correspondence with Jim Nowlan, various dates, 2011.

41. Susan Heathfield, "How to Change Your Culture: Organizational Culture Change," www.humanresources.about.com, 2012.

42. Robert F. Rich, "Public Learning: Transforming Beliefs and Attitudes," paper delivered at the Ethics and Reform Symposium, September 27–28, 2012, Chicago, pp. 23–24, and available from the Paul Simon Public Policy Institute, Southern Illinois University, Carbondale.

43. Dick Simpson, personal conversation with Jim Nowlan, undated.

44. Nowlan, *Glory, Darkness, Light*, chap. 5, "The Titan Versus the Second Class Businessman," pp. 42–45.

45. Charles E. Merriam, *Chicago: A More Intimate View of Urban Politics* (New York: MacMillan, 1929), p. 21.

46. Richard H. Thaler and Cass R. Sunstein, *Nudge: Improving Decisions About Health, Wealth, and Happiness* (London: Penguin, 2009), 60.

47. Ibid.

48. Beth A. Rosenson, *The Shadowlands of Conduct: Ethics and State Politics* (Washington, DC: Georgetown University Press, 2005), pp. 156–57.

49. Thomas J. Homer, Legislative Inspector General, letter to members of the Illinois General Assembly, Springfield, August 10, 2011.

50. Survey taken in January 2012 by the Northern Illinois University Center for Governmental Studies for the Illinois Integrity Initiative, Institute of Government and Public Affairs, University of Illinois, Urbana, January 2012.

Bibliographical Notes

This is a book of applied public policy. As such, the authors drew extensively on national as well as Illinois-based governmental and nongovernmental units that provide valuable research and analyses regarding issues related to Illinois. National organizations include the National Conference of State Legislatures, the Council of State Governments, the National Governors' Association, the Government Finance Officers' Association, the International City and County Managers Association, and *Governing* magazine.

Several Illinois government agencies that provided important information include the Commission on Government Forecasting and Accountability and the Legislative Research Unit, both of the Illinois General Assembly; the Office of the Comptroller, the Chicago Metropolitan Agency for Planning, and the Auditor General of Illinois.

University-based research and public service units include the Institute of Government and Public Affairs at the University of Illinois (especially for their annual Illinois Report), the Paul Simon Public Policy Institute at Southern Illinois University, the Center for Governmental Studies at Northern Illinois University, and the Illinois Institute for Rural Affairs at Western Illinois University.

Nongovernmental research-oriented organizations in Illinois include the Taxpayers' Federation of Illinois and its Illinois Fiscal Policy Council, the Civic Federation, the Center for Tax and Budget Accountability, the Illinois Policy Institute, and Advance Illinois (an education advocacy group).

An incomplete list of books that have proved instructive include the following:

Berry, Christopher R. *Imperfect Union: Representation and Taxation in Multilevel Governments*. Cambridge: Cambridge University Press, 2009.

Bogsnes, Bjarte. *Implementing Beyond Budgeting*. Hoboken, NJ: Wiley, 2008.

Callahan, Daniel. *Setting Limits: Medical Goals in an Aging Society*. Washington, DC: Georgetown University Press, 1995.

deBuys, William. *A Great Aridness: Climate Change and the Future of the American Southwest*. New York: Oxford University Press, 2011.

Florida, Richard. *Rise of the Creative Class*. New York: Basic, 2004.

Gold, Steven D., ed. *The Unfinished Agenda for State Tax Reform*. Denver: National Conference of State Legislatures, 1988.

Greenwood, Daphne T., and Richard P. F. Holt. *Local Economic Development in the 21st Century*. Armonk, NY: Sharpe, 2010.

Hughes, Jonathan, and Louis P. Cain. *American Economic History, 8th ed.* Upper Saddle River, NJ: Prentice Hall, 2011.

Hunt, D. Bradford, and Jon B. DeVries. *Planning Chicago*. Chicago: American Planning Association, 2013.

Kelly, Janet, and William Rivenbark. *Performance Budgeting for State and Local Government*. Armonk, NY: Sharpe, 2011.

Koval, John P., et al., eds. *The New Chicago: A Social and Cultural Analysis*. Philadelphia: Temple University Press, 2006.

Koven, Steven G., and Thomas S. Lyons. *Economic Development: Strategies for State and Local Practice*. Washington, DC: ICMA Press, 2010.

Longworth, Richard C. *Caught in the Middle: America's Heartland in the Age of Globalism*. New York: Bloomsbury USA, 2008.

Merriner, James L. *Grafters and Goo Goos: Corruption and Reform in Chicago, 1833–2003*. Carbondale: Southern Illinois University Press, 2004.

Nowlan, James D., Samuel K. Gove, and Richard J. Winkel Jr. *Illinois Politics: A Citizen's Guide*. Urbana: University of Illinois Press, 2010.

Osborne, David, and Peter Hutchinson. *The Price of Government: Getting Results We Need in an Age of Permanent Fiscal Crisis*. New York: Basic, 2004.

Rubin, Irene. *The Politics of Public Budgeting: Getting and Spending, Borrowing and Balancing*. 6th ed. Washington, DC: CQ, 2009.

Schweke, Bill. *A Progressive Economic Development Agenda for Shared Prosperity: Taking the High Road and Closing the Low*. Washington, DC: Corporation for Enterprise Development, 2006.

Seavoy, Ronald. *An Economic History of the United States from 1607 to the Present*. New York: Routledge Chapman & Hall, 2006.

Simpson, Dick, and Constance A. Mixon, eds. *Twenty-first Century Chicago*. 2d ed., rev. San Diego: Cognella, 2013.

Thaler, Richard H., and Cass Sunstein. *Nudge: Improving Decisions About Health, Wealth, and Happiness*. New York: Penguin, 2009.

Wu, Liangfu, and Larry Bury. *Introduction to Dynamic Government Performance Measurement*. Northwest Municipal Conference and CityTech USA, 2004. www.citytechusa.com/pdf/eMeasure.pdf.

Index

James Nowlan served two terms in the Illinois House of Representatives and worked under three governors. He is the coauthor of *Illinois Politics: A Citizen's Guide.*

J. Thomas Johnson was director of the Illinois Department of Revenue and is President Emeritus of the Taxpayers' Federation of Illinois.

The University of Illinois Press
is a founding member of the
Association of American University Presses.

Designed by Jim Proefrock
Composed in 10.5/13 Adobe Minion Pro
with Trade Gothic and Avenir display
at the University of Illinois Press
Manufactured by Sheridan Books, Inc.

University of Illinois Press
1325 South Oak Street
Champaign, IL 61820-6903
www.press.uillinois.edu